2016-2017

SUNDAY
MISSAL
for YOUNG
CATHOLICS

Living with Christ
Bayard, Inc.
1 Montauk Avenue, Suite 200
New London, CT 06320
860-437-3012 or 1-800-321-0411
www.livingwithchrist.us

 A DIVISION OF
BAYARD, INC.

LITURGICAL TEXTS:

The English translation of Psalm Responses, Conclusions to the Readings from Lectionary for
Mass © 1969, 1981, 1997, International Commission on English in the Liturgy Corporation (ICEL);
excerpts from the English translation of Eucharistic Prayers for Masses with Children © 1975,
ICEL; excerpts from the English translation of The Roman Missal © 2010, ICEL. All rights reserved.

Texts contained in this work derived whole or in part from liturgical texts copyrighted by the
International Commission on English in the Liturgy (ICEL) have been published here with the
confirmation of the Committee on Divine Worship, United States Conference of Catholic Bishops.
No other texts in this work have been formally reviewed or approved by the United States
Conference of Catholic Bishops.

ILLUSTRATIONS:

Olivier Balez; Brooke Kerrigan; Marcelino Truong

ISBN: 978-1-62785-158-9

Printed in Canada.

A Canadian edition of the *Missal for Young Catholics* is published by
Novalis Publishing Inc., 10 Lower Spadina Ave., Suite 400, Toronto, ON M5V 2Z2

2016-2017

SUNDAY MISSAL *for* YOUNG CATHOLICS

I want to know Jesus better.

This missal will help you take part in the Mass on Sundays and important feast days. Pages 4 to 32 contain the words and explain the gestures that are the same for every Mass. The rest of the book gives you the readings and prayers for each Sunday of the year.

Look over the readings with your family before you go to church. This is an excellent way to use this book and a wonderful way to prepare for Mass.

The most important thing about this little book is that it will help you to know Jesus better. Jesus came to bring God's love into the world. And his Spirit continues to fill us with love for one another.

We hope the short notes in this book will help you to participate more fully in the Mass. May the Mass become an important part of your life as you grow up, and may the readings and prayers you find in this missal inspire you to love and serve others just as Jesus did.

What We Need to Celebrate the Mass

The **priest** makes Jesus present and acts in his name.

The **altar** is the table where the priest consecrates bread and wine.

A group of Christians. You are a Christian by your baptism.

Two **books** are used at Mass: the missal contains the prayers of the Mass, and the lectionary contains the readings.

One **cruet** contains water, while the other cruet contains wine.

Holy vessels

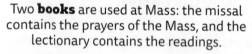

chalice   *ciborium*   *paten*

Bread and wine
The Mass is the commemoration of what Jesus did during the Last Supper with his disciples, before he died. The bread is shaped like a small disc and is called a "host."

The **ambo** is the place where the word of God is proclaimed.

The Four Main Parts of the Mass

On the following pages you will find the words that the priest says and the responses we say together during each part of the Mass. You will also find explanations and responses to many questions that people ask about the Mass.

The Introductory Rites

The Lord brings us together.
We ask God for forgiveness.
We give glory to God.

The Liturgy of the Word

We listen to the word of God.
We profess our faith.
We pray for the whole world.

The Liturgy of the Eucharist

We offer bread and wine to God.
We give thanks to God.
We say the Lord's Prayer.
We share the peace of Christ.
We receive Jesus in communion.

The Concluding Rites

The Lord sends us forth to live the Gospel.

The Lord Brings Us Together

We come together in church with family, friends, neighbors, and strangers. We are here because Jesus has invited us to be here.

When the priest comes in, we stand and sing. Then we make the sign of the cross along with the priest.

Priest: In the name of the Father, and of the Son, and of the Holy Spirit.

Everyone: Amen.

Sometimes, the words can change a bit, but usually the priest will say:

Priest: The grace of our Lord Jesus Christ, and the love of God, and the communion of the Holy Spirit be with you all.

Everyone: And with your spirit.

Questions

Why do we celebrate Mass on Sunday?
Jesus rose from the dead on Sunday, the day after the Sabbath. This is why Christians gather on that day. Over time, people started to call it "the Lord's day."

Why do we celebrate Mass in a church?
Churches are built specially for Christians to gather in. If needed, Mass can be celebrated in other places: a home, a school, a plaza, a jail, a hospital, a park...

Why do we need a priest to celebrate Mass?
We believe that Jesus is present in the person of the priest when Christians gather for the Mass. He presides over the celebration of the Lord's supper in the name of Jesus Christ.

Gestures

Standing
We stand to welcome Jesus, who is present among us when we gather in his name.

The sign of the cross
With our right hand we make the sign of the cross (from our forehead to our chest, from our left shoulder to our right) and say "In the name of the Father, and of the Son, and of the Holy Spirit." This is how most Catholic prayer begins.

Singing
This is a joyful way to pray together.

We Ask God for Forgiveness

We speak to God and we recognize that we have done wrong. We ask forgiveness for our misdeeds. God, who knows and loves us, forgives us.

Priest: Brothers and sisters, let us acknowledge our sins, and so prepare ourselves to celebrate the sacred mysteries.

We silently recognize our faults and allow God's loving forgiveness to touch us.

Everyone: I **confess** to almighty God
and to you, my brothers and sisters,
that I have greatly sinned,
in my thoughts and in my words,
in what I have done and in what I have failed to do,
(tap the heart) through my fault, through my fault,
through my most grievous fault;
therefore I ask blessed Mary ever-Virgin,
all the Angels and Saints,
and you, my brothers and sisters,
to pray for me to the Lord our God.

Priest: May almighty God have **mercy** on us, forgive us our sins, and bring us to everlasting life.

Everyone: **Amen.**

Priest: **Lord**, have mercy.

Everyone: Lord, have mercy.

Priest: **Christ**, have mercy.

Everyone: Christ, have mercy.

Priest: Lord, have mercy.

Everyone: Lord, have mercy.

What does it mean?

Confess
We recognize before others that we have turned away from God, who is love.

Mercy
We know God is full of mercy—that he loves us even when we have sinned. God's mercy is always there for us.

Amen
This is a Hebrew word meaning "Yes, I agree. I commit myself."

Lord
This is a name that we give to God. Christians call Jesus "Lord" because we believe he is the Son of God.

Christ or Messiah
In the Bible, these words designate someone who has been blessed with perfumed oil. This blessing is a sign that God has given a mission to the person. Christians give this name to Jesus.

Gestures

Tapping our heart
This is a way of showing we are very sorry for our sins.

9

We Give Glory to God

We recognize God's greatness when we say "Glory to God."
This prayer begins with the hymn the angels sang when they
announced Jesus' birth to the shepherds.

Everyone: **Glory** to God in the highest,
and on earth peace to people of good will.

We **praise** you,
we bless you,
we adore you,
we glorify you,
we give you thanks for your great glory,
Lord God, heavenly King,
O God, **almighty** Father.

Lord Jesus Christ, Only Begotten Son,
Lord God, Lamb of God, Son of the Father,
you take away the **sins of the world**,
    have mercy on us;
you take away the sins of the world,
    receive our prayer;
you are seated at the right hand of the Father,
    have mercy on us.

For you alone are the Holy One,
you alone are the Lord,
you alone are the Most High,
Jesus Christ,
with the **Holy Spirit**,
in the glory of God the Father.
Amen.

Priest: Let us pray.

*The priest invites us to pray. He then says a prayer
in the name of all of us, and finishes like this:*

Through our Lord Jesus Christ, your Son, who lives
and reigns with you in the unity of the Holy Spirit,
one God, for ever and ever.

Everyone: Amen.

What does it mean?

Glory
With this word, we indicate the greatness of a person. It shows that a person is important. When we say "Glory to God" we are recognizing that God is important in our lives.

Praise
To praise is to speak well and enthusiastically of someone.

Almighty
When we say that God is almighty, we mean that nothing is impossible for God.

Sins of the world
This expression refers to all the evil that is done in the world.

Holy Spirit
This is the Spirit of God, our heavenly guide, who fills us with love for Jesus.

We Listen to the Word of God

This is the moment when we listen to several readings from the **Bible**. We welcome God who speaks to us today.

You can follow the readings in this book. Look for the Sunday that corresponds to the day's date.

THE FIRST TWO READINGS

We sit down for these readings. The first reading is usually taken from the Old Testament. The second is from a letter written by an apostle to the first Christians. Between these two readings, we pray with the responsorial **Psalm**, *which we do best when it is sung.*

THE GOSPEL

We stand and sing **Alleluia!** *(except during Lent) as we prepare to listen carefully to a reading from one of the Gospels.*

Priest: The Lord be with you.

Everyone: And with your spirit.

Priest: A reading from the holy **Gospel** according to N.

Everyone: Glory to you, O Lord.

We trace three small crosses with our thumb: one on our forehead, one on our lips, and another on our heart. When the reading is finished, the priest kisses the book and says:

Priest: The Gospel of the Lord.

Everyone: Praise to you, Lord Jesus Christ.

THE HOMILY

We sit down to listen to the comments of the priest, which help us to understand and apply the word of God in our lives.

What does it mean?

Bible
This is the holy book of all Christians. The Old Testament tells the story of the covenant God made with the Jewish people before Jesus' time. The New Testament tells the story of the covenant God made with all people through his son, Jesus Christ.

Psalm
The Psalms are prayers that are found in the Bible. They are meant to be sung.

Alleluia!
This Hebrew word means "May God be praised and thanked."

Gospel
The word "gospel" means "good news." Jesus himself is the Good News who lives with us. The first four books of the New Testament are called "gospels." They transmit the good news to us.

Gestures

The sign of the cross which we make on our forehead, lips and heart
This sign means that we want to make the gospel so much a part of our life that we can proclaim it to all around us with all our being.

Kissing the book of the Gospels
When the priest does this, he says in a low voice: "Through the words of the gospel may our sins be wiped away."

We Profess Our Faith

We have just listened to the word of God. To respond to it, we proclaim the **Creed**.

We stand up and profess our faith:

Everyone:
I believe in one God,
the Father almighty,
maker of heaven and earth,
of all things visible and invisible.

I believe in one Lord Jesus Christ,
the Only Begotten Son of God,
born of the Father before all ages.
God from God, Light from Light,
true God from true God,
begotten, not made, consubstantial with the Father;
through him all things were made.
For us men and for our salvation
he came down from heaven,
*(At the words that follow, up to and including
"and became man," all bow.)*
and by the Holy Spirit was incarnate of the Virgin Mary,
and became man.

For our sake he was **crucified** under **Pontius Pilate**,
he suffered death and was buried,
and rose again on the third day
in accordance with the Scriptures.
He ascended into heaven
and is seated at the right hand of the Father.
He will come again in glory
to judge the living and the dead
and his kingdom will have no end.

I believe in the Holy Spirit, the Lord, the giver of life,
who proceeds from the Father and the Son,
who with the Father and the Son is adored and glorified,
who has spoken through the prophets.

I believe in one, holy, **catholic** and apostolic **Church**.
I confess one Baptism for the forgiveness of sins
and I look forward to the **resurrection** of the dead
and the life of the world to come. Amen.

What does it mean?

Creed
From the Latin verb *credo*, meaning "I believe." The Creed is the prayer that expresses our faith as Christians.

Crucified
Jesus died by crucifixion, meaning he was nailed to a cross.

Pontius Pilate
This is the name of the Roman governor who ordered that Jesus be crucified.

Catholic
In Greek, this word means "universal." The Church is open to all people in the world.

Church
The "Church" with a big C refers to the whole Christian community throughout the world. The "church" with a little c is a building where we gather to worship God.

Resurrection
This means coming back to life after having died. God raised Jesus from the dead and gave him new life for ever. Jesus shares that life with us.

We Pray for the Whole World

This is the moment of the Universal Prayer of the Faithful when we present our **petitions** to God. We pray for the Church, for all of humanity, for those who are sick or lonely, for children who are abandoned, for those who suffer through natural disasters...

After each petition we respond with a phrase, such as:

Everyone: Lord, hear our prayer.

Reader: For the needs of the Church...

For peace in every country...

For the hungry and the homeless...

For ourselves and for all God's children...

What does it mean?

Petitions

Petitions are prayers asking for something specific. Each week at Mass, the petitions change because the needs of the world and our community change. We stand for the petitions and answer "Amen" at the end. Sometimes we call these prayers intentions.

Why do we call the Prayer of the Faithful "universal"?

It is a universal prayer because it includes everyone: we pray for all the people of the world.

Why do we take up a collection?

Christians help out with the maintenance of the church building and also help people who are in need. These gifts are brought to the altar with the bread and the wine.

We Offer Bread and Wine to God

The celebration of the Lord's Supper continues at the altar. Members of the community bring the bread, the wine, and the gifts collected to relieve the needs of the Church and the poor. The priest receives the gifts and then with him we bless God for the bread and wine that will become the Body and Blood of Jesus.

We sit down. The priest takes the bread and wine, and lifts them up, saying:

Priest: **Blessed** are you, Lord God of all creation, for through your goodness we have received the bread we offer you: fruit of the earth and work of human hands, it will become for us the bread of life.

Everyone: Blessed be God for ever.

Priest: Blessed are you, Lord God of all creation, for through your goodness we have received the wine we offer you: fruit of the vine and work of human hands, it will become our spiritual drink.

Everyone: Blessed be God for ever.

The priest washes his hands. Then we all stand and the priest says:

Priest: Pray, brothers and sisters, that my sacrifice and yours may be acceptable to God, the almighty Father.

Everyone: May the Lord accept the **sacrifice** at your hands for the praise and glory of his name, for our good, and the good of all his holy Church.

The priest, with hands extended, says a prayer over the bread and wine. He usually ends the prayer by saying:

Priest: Through Christ our Lord.

Everyone: Amen.

What does it mean?

Eucharist
A Greek word that means "gratefulness, thanksgiving." The Mass is also called the Eucharist.

Blessed
To bless means to speak well of someone. To bless God is to give thanks for everything God gives us.

Sacrifice
God does not ask for animal sacrifice, as in the old days written about in the Bible. Nor does God ask us to die on a cross, like Jesus did. Instead, God asks us to offer our daily life, with Jesus, as a beautiful gift.

Gestures

Procession with the bread and the wine
With this gesture we present to God the fruit of our work and we give thanks for the gift of life that comes from God.

Drops of water in the wine
With this sign, the priest prays that our life be united with God's life.

Washing of hands
Before saying the most important prayer of the Mass, the priest washes his hands and asks God to wash away his sins.

We Give Thanks to God

At this moment we give thanks to God for his Son, Jesus Christ, for life, and for all that he gives us. This is how the great Eucharistic Prayer begins.

Priest: The Lord be with you.

Everyone: And with your spirit.

Priest: Lift up your hearts.

Everyone: We lift them up to the Lord.

Priest: Let us give thanks to the Lord our God.

Everyone: It is right and just.

Here is one way of celebrating the Eucharist with young Catholics. On page 23, you will find Eucharistic Prayer II, which is a common way of celebrating the Eucharist with grown-ups.

Eucharistic Prayer for Masses with Children I

Priest: God our Father,
you have brought us here together
so that we can give you thanks and praise
for all the wonderful things you have done.

We thank you for all that is beautiful in the world
and for the happiness you have given us.
We praise you for daylight
and for your word which lights up our minds.
We praise you for the earth,
and all the people who live on it,
and for our life which comes from you.

We know that you are good.
You love us and do great things for us.

So we all sing together:

Everyone: Holy, Holy, Holy Lord God of hosts.
Heaven and earth are full of your glory.
Hosanna in the highest.

Priest: Father,
you are always thinking about your people;
you never forget us.
You sent us your Son Jesus,
who gave his life for us
and who came to save us.
He cured sick people;
he cared for those who were poor
and wept with those who were sad.
He forgave sinners
and taught us to forgive each other.
He loved everyone
and showed us how to be kind.
He took children in his arms and blessed them.

So we are glad to sing:

Everyone: Blessed is he who comes in the name of the Lord.
Hosanna in the highest.

Priest: God our Father,
all over the world your people praise you.
So now we pray with the whole Church:
with N., our Pope and N., our Bishop.
In heaven the Blessed Virgin Mary,
the Apostles and all the Saints
always sing your praise.
Now we join with them and with the Angels
to adore you as we sing:

Everyone: Holy, Holy, Holy Lord God of hosts.
Heaven and earth are full of your glory.
Hosanna in the highest.
Blessed is he who comes in the name of the Lord.
Hosanna in the highest.

Priest: God our Father,
you are most holy
and we want to show you that we are grateful.
We bring you bread and wine
and ask you to send your Holy Spirit
    to make these gifts
the Body and Blood of Jesus your Son.
Then we can offer to you
what you have given to us.

On the night before he died,
Jesus was having supper with his Apostles.
He took bread from the table.
He gave you thanks and praise.
Then he broke the bread,
gave it to his friends, and said:

> TAKE THIS, ALL OF YOU, AND EAT OF IT,
> FOR THIS IS MY BODY
> WHICH WILL BE GIVEN UP FOR YOU.

When supper was ended,
Jesus took the chalice that was filled with wine.
He thanked you, gave it to his friends, and said:

> TAKE THIS, ALL OF YOU, AND DRINK FROM IT,
> FOR THIS IS THE CHALICE OF MY BLOOD,
> THE BLOOD OF THE NEW AND ETERNAL **COVENANT**,
> WHICH WILL BE POURED OUT FOR YOU AND FOR MANY
> FOR THE **FORGIVENESS OF SINS.**

Then he said to them:

> DO THIS IN MEMORY OF ME.

We do now what Jesus told us to do.
We remember his Death
and his Resurrection
and we offer you, Father,
the bread that gives us life,
and the chalice that saves us.
Jesus brings us to you;
welcome us as you welcome him.

Let us proclaim our faith:

Everyone: We proclaim your Death, O Lord,
and profess your Resurrection
until you come again.

or

When we eat this Bread and drink this Cup,
we proclaim your Death, O Lord,
until you come again.

or

Save us, Savior of the world,
for by your Cross and Resurrection
you have set us free.

Priest: Father,
because you love us,
you invite us to come to your table.
Fill us with the joy of the Holy Spirit
as we receive the Body and Blood of your Son.

Lord,
you never forget any of your children.
We ask you to take care of those we love,
especially of N. and N.,
and we pray for those who have died.
Remember everyone who is suffering
from pain or sorrow.

Remember Christians everywhere
and all other people in the world.

We are filled with wonder and praise
when we see what you do for us
through Jesus your Son,
and so we give you praise.

Through him, and with him, and in him,
O God, almighty Father,
in the unity of the Holy Spirit,
all glory and honor is yours,
for ever and ever.

Everyone: Amen.

(Turn to page 27)

Eucharistic Prayer II

Priest: It is truly right and just, our duty and our salvation,
always and everywhere to give you thanks,
    Father most holy,
through your beloved Son, Jesus Christ,
your Word through whom you made all things,
whom you sent as our Savior and Redeemer,
incarnate by the Holy Spirit and born of the Virgin.

Fulfilling your will and gaining for you a holy people,
he stretched out his hands
as he endured his Passion,
so as to break the bonds of death and manifest
    the resurrection.

And so, with the Angels and all the Saints
we declare your glory,
as with one voice we acclaim:

Everyone: Holy, Holy, Holy Lord God of hosts.
Heaven and earth are full of your glory.
Hosanna in the highest.
Blessed is he who comes in the name of the Lord.
Hosanna in the highest.

Priest: You are indeed Holy, O Lord,
the fount of all holiness.

Make holy, therefore, these gifts, we pray,
by sending down your Spirit upon them like the dewfall,
so that they may become for us
the Body and Blood of our Lord Jesus Christ.

At the time he was betrayed
and entered willingly into his Passion,
he took bread and, giving thanks, broke it,
and gave it to his disciples, saying:

> TAKE THIS, ALL OF YOU, AND EAT OF IT,
> FOR THIS IS MY BODY
> WHICH WILL BE GIVEN UP FOR YOU.

In a similar way,
>> when supper was ended,
>> he took the chalice
>> and, once more giving thanks,
>> he gave it to his disciples, saying:

>>> TAKE THIS, ALL OF YOU, AND DRINK FROM IT,
>>> FOR THIS IS THE CHALICE OF MY BLOOD,
>>> THE BLOOD OF THE NEW AND ETERNAL **COVENANT**,
>>> WHICH WILL BE POURED OUT FOR YOU AND FOR MANY
>>> FOR THE **FORGIVENESS OF SINS**.

>>> **DO THIS IN MEMORY OF ME.**

>> **The mystery of faith.**

Everyone: We proclaim your Death, O Lord,
and profess your Resurrection
until you come again.

or

When we eat this Bread and drink this Cup,
we proclaim your Death, O Lord,
until you come again.

or

Save us, Savior of the world,
for by your Cross and Resurrection
you have set us free.

Priest: Therefore, as we celebrate
the **memorial** of his Death and Resurrection,
we offer you, Lord,
the Bread of life and the Chalice of salvation,
giving thanks that you have held us worthy
to be in your presence and minister to you.

Humbly we pray
that, partaking of the Body and Blood of Christ,
we may be gathered into one by the Holy Spirit.
Remember, Lord, your Church,
spread throughout the world,
and bring her to the fullness of charity,
together with N. our Pope and N. our Bishop
and all the clergy.

Remember also our brothers and sisters
who have fallen asleep in the hope of the resurrection,
and all who have died in your mercy:
welcome them into the light of your face.
Have mercy on us all, we pray,
that with the Blessed Virgin Mary, Mother of God,
with blessed Joseph, her Spouse,
with the blessed Apostles, and all the Saints
who have pleased you throughout the ages,
we may merit to be co-heirs to **eternal life**,
and may praise and glorify you
through your Son, Jesus Christ.

Through him, and with him, and in him,
O God, almighty Father,
in the unity of the Holy Spirit,
all glory and honor is yours,
for ever and ever.

Everyone: Amen.

Gestures

Extending the hands
When the priest extends his hands, he calls upon the Holy Spirit to consecrate the bread and wine, so that they become for us the Body and Blood of Christ.

Raising the bread
The priest lifts the consecrated bread and then the chalice, so that the community may see and respectfully adore the Body and Blood of Christ.

Kneeling
This is a common way to show respect and to worship.

What does it mean?

Covenant

When two people enter into a covenant, they promise to be faithful to one another. God entered into a covenant with us. He is our God and we are his People.

Forgiveness of sins

This is the forgiveness that comes from God, whose love is greater than our sins.

Do this in memory of me

Jesus asked the disciples to remember him by reliving what he said and did during the Last Supper.

Memorial

Memorial means to remember. When we remember at Mass, we're not just thinking about something that happened a long time ago. To remember Jesus' death and resurrection at Mass means that those events are real and happening now, in our celebration, in our hearts. It doesn't mean that Jesus is repeating his passion, death, and resurrection for us at each Mass, but that, at each Mass, the Holy Spirit makes the powerful saving mystery of Jesus' death and resurrection present to us. No one can explain this or fully understand it. It is part of the mystery of faith.

We may be gathered into one by the Holy Spirit

In the Mass, the Holy Spirit draws us into unity—communion—not only with Jesus, but with all the members of his body—with the pope and our bishop and all the bishops and clergy, with every member of the Church throughout the world, with all members of the body of Christ who share in eternal life, including the Blessed Virgin Mary, the apostles, and all the saints. When we gather at Mass, even though we can't see them, we know in faith that the whole body of Christ is with us praising and worshiping God.

The mystery of faith

Together we proclaim our belief in Christ who was born and died for us, rose to life, and will return one day.

Eternal life

This is life with God, which will be given to us fully after death.

We Say the Lord's Prayer

Jesus has taught us that God is the Father of all human beings and that we can call upon God at any time. Together we recite or sing this prayer. To help us to be truly ready to receive Jesus in Communion, we need to ask for forgiveness and to forgive those who have hurt us.

Priest: At the **Savior's** command and formed by divine teaching, we dare to say:

Everyone: Our Father,
who art in **heaven**,
hallowed be thy name;
thy kingdom come,
thy will be done
on earth as it is in heaven.
Give us this day our daily bread,
and forgive us our **trespasses**,
as we forgive those who trespass against us;
and lead us not into **temptation**,
but deliver us from evil.

Priest: Deliver us, Lord, we pray, from every evil, graciously grant peace in our days, that, by the help of your mercy, we may be always free from sin and safe from all distress, as we await the blessed hope and the coming of our Savior, Jesus Christ.

Everyone: For the **kingdom**,
the power and the glory are yours
now and for ever.

What does it mean?

Savior

This is one of the names we give to Jesus because he saves us from evil and death.

Heaven

Heaven is a special way of being with God after our life on earth is over.

Trespasses

These refer to our lack of love and to the sins we commit.

Temptation

This is a desire we sometimes feel to do things we know are wrong.

Kingdom

Jesus speaks of God as king when he says: "The kingdom of God is at hand." With his life, Jesus shows us that God is present in our midst as a king who loves us. When we live as Jesus did, we welcome the kingdom of God.

We Share the Peace of Christ

God is our Father and we are brothers and sisters in Christ. In order to show that we are one family, the priest invites us to offer each other a sign of peace.

Priest: Lord Jesus Christ, who said to your Apostles: Peace I leave you, my peace I give you, look not on our sins, but on the faith of your Church, and graciously grant her peace and **unity** in accordance with your will. Who live and reign for ever and ever.

Everyone: Amen.

Priest: The peace of the Lord be with you always.

Everyone: And with your spirit.

Priest: Let us offer each other the sign of peace.

At this time, by a handshake, a hug, or a bow, we give to those near us a sign of Christ's peace. Immediately after, we sing or say:

Everyone: **Lamb of God**, you take away the sins of the world, have mercy on us.

Lamb of God, you take away the sins of the world, have mercy on us.

Lamb of God, you take away the sins of the world, grant us peace.

What does it mean?

Unity

When we get together each Sunday to celebrate the Lord's Supper, we recognize our unity, or oneness, since we are all children of the same loving Father.

Lamb of God

In the Old Testament, believers offered a lamb to God. We call Jesus the Lamb of God because he offers his life to God.

Gestures

The sign of peace

We shake hands, hug or bow to one another to share the peace that comes from Christ. It is a sign of our commitment to live in peace with others.

We Receive Jesus in Communion

When we receive communion, the Bread of Life, Jesus feeds us with his very self.

The priest breaks the host and says:

Priest: Behold the Lamb of God,
behold him who takes away the sins of the world.
Blessed are those called to the supper of the Lamb.

Everyone: Lord, I am not worthy
that you should enter under my roof,
but only say the word
and my soul shall be healed.

It is time to come up to receive communion. The priest or the communion minister says:

Priest: The Body of Christ.

Everyone: Amen.

Questions

Why do we go to communion?

When we eat the bread, we receive Jesus. He gives himself to us this way so we can live for God. Sharing the Body and Blood of Christ in communion creates among us a special "one-ness" with God and with each other.

Why is the bread we share during Mass called a "host"?

The word "host" means "victim who is offered." The consecrated host is Jesus Christ, who offers himself in order to give life to others.

Gestures

The priest breaks the bread

The priest breaks the bread in the same way that Jesus did during the Last Supper, in order to share it. The early Christians used to call the Mass "the breaking of the bread."

Receiving the host

The priest or communion minister places the host in your left hand. Pick the host up with your right hand, put it in your mouth, eat the bread carefully, and return to your place. You take a few moments of quiet prayer to thank God for this Bread of Life.

The Lord Sends Us Forth

After announcements, the priest blesses us in the name of God. We are then sent to live out our faith among all the people we meet during the week.

Priest: The Lord be with you.

Everyone: And with your spirit.

Priest: May almighty God bless you, the Father, and the Son, and the Holy Spirit.

Everyone: Amen.

Then the priest sends us out, saying this or something similar:

Priest: Go in peace, glorifying the Lord by your life.

Everyone: Thanks be to God.

What does it mean?

The word "Mass"
The word "Mass" comes from the second word in the Latin phrase that was once used by the priest to announce the end of the Sunday celebration: *Ite missa est* — Go forth, the Mass is ended.

Communion for the sick
Sometimes people who are sick cannot be present at Sunday Mass. Communion ministers can take consecrated hosts to the homes of sick people so that they can receive communion and be assured that the rest of the community is praying for them.

Gestures

Blessing
The priest makes the sign of the cross over the people in church. With this blessing we are sent out with the loving strength of God to live a life of love and service to others.

Dismissal
We cannot stay together in the church all week. When the Mass is ended, we must go our separate ways, in peace and love, to witness to the risen Jesus in the world today.

First Reading *(Isaiah 2:1-5)*

This is what Isaiah, son of Amoz, saw concerning Judah and
Jerusalem.

In days to come,
the mountain of the Lord's house
shall be established as the highest mountain
and raised above the hills.
All nations shall stream toward it;
many peoples shall come and say:
"Come, let us climb the LORD's mountain,
to the house of the God of Jacob,
that he may instruct us in his ways,
and we may walk in his paths."
For from Zion shall go forth instruction,
and the word of the LORD from Jerusalem.
He shall judge between the nations,
and impose terms on many peoples.
They shall beat their swords into plowshares
and their spears into pruning hooks;
one nation shall not raise the sword against another,
nor shall they train for war again.
O **house of Jacob**, come,
let us walk in the light of the LORD!

The word of the Lord. **Thanks be to God.**

Responsorial Psalm *(Psalm 122:1-2, 3-4, 4-5, 6-7, 8-9)*

R. **Let us go rejoicing to the house of the Lord.**

I rejoiced because they said to me,
"We will go up to the house of the LORD."
And now we have set foot
within your gates, O Jerusalem. R.
Jerusalem, built as a city
with compact unity.
To it the tribes go up,
the tribes of the LORD. R.
According to the decree for Israel,
to give thanks to the name of the LORD.
In it are set up judgment seats,
seats for the house of David. R.

Pray for the peace of Jerusalem!
    May those who love you prosper!
May peace be within your walls,
    prosperity in your buildings. R̲.
Because of my brothers and friends
    I will say, "Peace be within you!"
Because of the house of the LORD, our God,
    I will pray for your good. R̲.

Second Reading *(Romans 13:11-14)*

Brothers and sisters: You know the time; it is the hour now for you to awake from sleep. For our salvation is nearer now than when we first believed; the night is advanced, the day is at hand. Let us then throw off the **works of darkness** and put on the **armor of light**; let us conduct ourselves properly as in the day, not in orgies and drunkenness, not in promiscuity and lust, not in rivalry and jealousy. But put on the Lord Jesus Christ, and make no provision for the desires of the flesh.

The word of the Lord. **Thanks be to God.**

Gospel *(Matthew 24:37-44)*

A reading from the holy Gospel according to Matthew.
Glory to you, O Lord.

Jesus said to his disciples: "As it was in the days of **Noah**, so it will be at the coming of the Son of Man. In those days before the flood, they were eating and drinking, marrying and giving in marriage, up to the day that Noah entered the ark. They did not know until the flood came and carried them all away. So will it be also at the coming of the Son of Man. Two men will be out in the field; one will be taken, and one will be left. Two women will be grinding at the mill; one will be taken, and one will be left. Therefore, **stay awake**! For you do not know on which day your Lord will come. Be sure of this: if the master of the house had known the hour of night when the thief was coming, he would have stayed awake and not let his house be broken into. So too, you also must be prepared, for at an hour you do not expect, the Son of Man will come."

The Gospel of the Lord. **Praise to you, Lord Jesus Christ.**

When the prophet Isaiah speaks of **the mountain of the Lord's house**, he is referring to the temple of Jerusalem. In saying it is the highest of the mountains, Isaiah wants to communicate that there will come a time when the God of Israel will be known and revered by all the people of the world.

Jacob was a grandson of Abraham and father of twelve sons, after whom the twelve tribes of Israel were named. The **house of Jacob** was another way to refer to all the people of Israel.

The **works of darkness** are bad actions that break our friendship with God and other people. We prefer to keep them hidden or out of the light, because we're not proud of what we have done.

The **armor of light** is our willingness and desire to follow the teachings of Jesus. To be friends of Jesus we must be ready to struggle against all that might distance us from God.

Noah was the just man chosen by God to be saved from the flood, along with his family and two of every animal. God asked Noah to build a huge boat, called an ark, in which he, his family, and the animals lived during the flood.

To **stay awake** is to avoid sleep throughout the night. But it also means to be alert so that nothing can surprise us. Christians must live in such a way that we're ready at any moment to meet our Lord.

First Reading *(Isaiah 11:1-10)*

On that day, a **shoot** shall sprout from the stump of Jesse,
    and from his roots a bud shall blossom.
The spirit of the LORD shall rest upon him:
    a spirit of wisdom and of understanding,
a spirit of counsel and of strength,
    a spirit of knowledge and of **fear of the LORD**,
    and his delight shall be the fear of the LORD.
Not by appearance shall he judge,
    nor by hearsay shall he decide,
but he shall judge the poor with justice,
    and decide aright for the land's afflicted.
He shall strike the ruthless with the rod of his mouth,
    and with the breath of his lips he shall slay the wicked.
Justice shall be the band around his waist,
    and faithfulness a belt upon his hips.
Then the wolf shall be a guest of the lamb,
    and the leopard shall lie down with the kid;
the calf and the young lion shall browse together,
    with a little child to guide them.
The cow and the bear shall be neighbors,
    together their young shall rest;
    the lion shall eat hay like the ox.
The baby shall play by the cobra's den,
    and the child lay his hand on the adder's lair.
There shall be no harm or ruin on all my holy mountain;
    for the earth shall be filled with knowledge of the LORD,
    as water covers the sea.
On that day, the root of Jesse,
    set up as a signal for the nations,
the Gentiles shall seek out,
    for his dwelling shall be glorious.

The word of the Lord. **Thanks be to God.**

Responsorial Psalm *(Psalm 72:1-2, 7-8, 12-13, 17)*

R. **Justice shall flourish in his time,
and fullness of peace forever.**

O God, with your judgment endow the king,
    and with your justice, the king's son;
he shall govern your people with justice
    and your afflicted ones with judgment. R.
Justice shall flower in his days,
    and profound peace, till the moon be no more.
May he rule from sea to sea,
    and from the River to the ends of the earth. R.
For he shall rescue the poor when he cries out,
    and the afflicted when he has no one to help him.
He shall have pity for the lowly and the poor;
    the lives of the poor he shall save. R.
May his name be blessed forever;
    as long as the sun his name shall remain.
In him shall all the tribes of the earth be blessed;
    all the nations shall proclaim his happiness. R.

Second Reading *(Romans 15:4-9)*

Brothers and sisters: Whatever was written previously was written for our instruction, that by endurance and by the encouragement of the Scriptures we might have **hope**. May the God of endurance and encouragement grant you to think in harmony with one another, in keeping with Christ Jesus, that with one accord you may with one voice glorify the God and Father of our Lord Jesus Christ.

Welcome one another, then, as Christ welcomed you, for the glory of God. For I say that Christ became a minister of the circumcised to show God's truthfulness, to confirm the promises to **the patriarchs**, but so that the Gentiles might glorify God for his mercy. As it is written:

*Therefore, I will praise you among the Gentiles
    and sing praises to your name.*

The word of the Lord. **Thanks be to God.**

Gospel *(Matthew 3:1-12)*

A reading from the holy Gospel according to Matthew.
Glory to you, O Lord.

John the Baptist appeared, preaching in the desert of Judea and saying, "Repent, for the kingdom of heaven is at hand!" It was of him that the prophet Isaiah had spoken when he said:

A voice of one crying out in the desert,
Prepare the way of the Lord,
make straight his paths.

John wore clothing made of camel's hair and had a leather belt around his waist. His food was locusts and wild honey. At that time Jerusalem, all Judea, and the whole region around the Jordan were going out to him and were being baptized by him in the Jordan River as they acknowledged their sins.

When he saw many of the **Pharisees** and **Sadducees** coming to his baptism, he said to them, "You brood of vipers! Who warned you to flee from the coming wrath? Produce good fruit as evidence of your repentance. And do not presume to say to yourselves, 'We have Abraham as our father.' For I tell you, God can raise up children to Abraham from these stones. Even now the ax lies at the root of the trees. Therefore every tree that does not bear good fruit will be cut down and thrown into the fire. I am baptizing you with water, for repentance, but the one who is coming after me is mightier than I. I am **not worthy to carry his sandals**. He will baptize you with the Holy Spirit and fire. His winnowing fan is in his hand. He will clear his threshing floor and gather his wheat into his barn, but the chaff he will burn with unquenchable fire."

The Gospel of the Lord.
Praise to you, Lord Jesus Christ.

When the prophet Isaiah speaks of a **shoot** coming out from the stump of Jesse, he is making a comparison between a branch that seems withered and dead, and the hope and new life of the people. When Isaiah refers to the appearance of a branch growing from the roots of Jesse, he is referring to Jesus who is descended from Jesse.

To have the spirit of **fear of the Lord** does not mean to be afraid of God. Rather, it signifies having a heart that is full of respect for the greatness of the Creator.

Hope is the confidence we have as Christians that God will always support us. God made this promise in many ways, but especially when he sent us his son, Jesus Christ.

The patriarchs are the ancestors of the people of Israel. Abraham, Isaac and Jacob were all known by this name. They received God's promise that his people would become a great nation.

John the Baptist was the son of Zechariah and Elizabeth, who was a cousin of the Virgin Mary. He preached the coming of the Messiah. He was called John the Baptist because those who were converted by his preaching were baptized in order to prepare themselves for the coming of the Savior.

The **Pharisees** and the **Sadducees** were people who belonged to two Jewish religious sects. Pharisees were very strict and believed religion consisted in obeying the rules, sometimes forgetting that love is the greatest rule. The Sadducees did not believe in the resurrection of the dead.

When one person was recognized as being much less important than another, it was said they were **not worthy to carry his sandals**. Untying and carrying the sandals of a visitor was a job for a slave; if you are not worthy even to do the work of a slave, then the important person is very great indeed.

41

DECEMBER 8
The Immaculate Conception of the Blessed Virgin Mary

First Reading *(Genesis 3:9-15, 20)*

After the man, **Adam**, had eaten of the tree, the LORD God called to the man and asked him, "Where are you?" He answered, "I heard you in the garden; but I was afraid, because I was naked, so I hid myself." Then he asked, "Who told you that you were naked? You have eaten, then, from the tree of which I had forbidden you to eat!" The man replied, "The woman whom you put here with me—she gave me fruit from the tree, and so I ate it." The LORD God then asked the woman, "Why did you do such a thing?" The woman answered, "The serpent tricked me into it, so I ate it."

   Then the LORD God said to the serpent:
   "Because you have done this, you shall be banned
      from all the animals
      and from all the wild creatures;
   on your belly shall you crawl,
      and dirt shall you eat
      all the days of your life.
   I will put enmity between you and the woman,
      and between your offspring and hers;
   he will strike at your head,
      while you strike at his heel."

The man called his wife **Eve**, because she became the mother of all the living.

The word of the Lord. **Thanks be to God.**

Responsorial Psalm *(Psalm 98:1, 2-3ab, 3cd-4)*

R. **Sing to the Lord a new song, for he has done marvelous deeds.**

Sing to the LORD a new song,
   for he has done wondrous deeds;
His right hand has won victory for him,
   his holy arm. R.
The LORD has made his salvation known:
   in the sight of the nations he has revealed his justice.
He has remembered his kindness and his faithfulness
   toward the house of Israel. R.
All the ends of the earth have seen
   the salvation by our God.
Sing joyfully to the LORD, all you lands;
   break into song; sing praise. R.

Second Reading *(Ephesians 1:3-6, 11-12)*

Brothers and sisters: Blessed be the God and Father of our Lord Jesus Christ, who has blessed us in Christ with every spiritual blessing in the heavens, as he chose us in him, before the foundation of the world, to be holy and without blemish before him. In love he destined us for **adoption** to himself through Jesus Christ, in accord with the favor of his will, for the praise of the glory of his grace that he granted us in the beloved.

In him we were also chosen, destined in accord with the purpose of the One who accomplishes all things according to the intention of his will, so that we might exist for the praise of his glory, we who first hoped in Christ.

The word of the Lord. **Thanks be to God.**

Gospel *(Luke 1:26-38)*

A reading from the holy Gospel according to Luke.
Glory to you, O Lord.

The angel Gabriel was sent from God to a town of Galilee called Nazareth, to a virgin betrothed to a man named Joseph, of the house of David, and the virgin's name was Mary. And coming to her, he said, "Hail, full of grace! The Lord is with you." But she was greatly troubled at what was said and pondered what sort of greeting this might be. Then the angel said to her, "Do not be afraid, Mary, for you have found favor with God. Behold, you will conceive in your womb and bear a son, and you shall name him Jesus. He will be great and will be called Son of the Most High, and the Lord God will give him the throne of David his father, and he will rule over the house of Jacob forever, and of his Kingdom there will be no end." But Mary said to the angel, "How can this be, since I have no relations with a man?" And the angel said to her in reply, "The Holy Spirit will come upon you, and the power of the Most High will overshadow you. Therefore the child to be born will be called holy, the Son of God. And behold, Elizabeth, your relative, has also conceived a son in her old age, and this is the sixth month for her who was called barren; for nothing will be impossible for God." Mary said, "Behold, I am the handmaid of the Lord. May it be done to me according to your word." Then the angel departed from her.

The Gospel of the Lord. **Praise to you, Lord Jesus Christ.**

The **Immaculate Conception** is the day we remember that God kept the Virgin Mary free from sin from the very beginning of her life. God did this for Mary because she was the mother of our Savior, Jesus, and it is through Jesus that all of us, including Mary, are redeemed and saved from sin.

Some stories are true on the inside, even if they are not completely true on the outside. The Church does not teach that the story of **Adam** and **Eve** happened just as it is told in this reading. But it does teach that this story tells us a very important truth about how human beings first turned away from God—and often still do.

When God says "**he will strike at your head**," the Church believes that God is speaking about Jesus, who will come and save human beings from sin.

Children without parents can be adopted into new families. A similar process of **adoption** happened in our baptism. Through baptism, we have been adopted by God, our heavenly parent. We have become brothers and sisters of Jesus, and brothers and sisters to one another, all of us children of God, called to share God's love and life.

First Reading *(Isaiah 35:1-6a, 10)*

The desert and the parched land will exult;
   the steppe will rejoice and bloom.
They will bloom with abundant flowers,
   and rejoice with joyful song.
The glory of **Lebanon** will be given to them,
   the splendor of **Carmel** and **Sharon**;
they will see the glory of the LORD,
   the splendor of our God.
Strengthen the hands that are feeble,
   make firm the knees that are weak,
say to those whose hearts are frightened:
   Be strong, fear not!
Here is your God,
   he comes with vindication;
with divine recompense
   he comes to save you.
Then will the eyes of the blind be opened,
   the ears of the deaf be cleared;
then will the lame leap like a stag,
   then the tongue of the mute will sing.
Those whom the LORD has ransomed will return
   and enter Zion singing,
   crowned with everlasting joy;
they will meet with joy and gladness,
   sorrow and mourning will flee.

The word of the Lord. **Thanks be to God.**

Responsorial Psalm *(Psalm 146:6-7, 8-9, 9-10)*

R. **Lord, come and save us.** *Or* **Alleluia!**

The LORD God keeps faith forever,
 secures justice for the **oppressed**,
 gives food to the hungry.
The LORD sets captives free. R.
The LORD gives sight to the blind;
 the Lord raises up those who were bowed down.
The Lord loves the just;
 the LORD protects strangers. R.
The fatherless and the widow he sustains,
 but the way of the wicked he thwarts.
The LORD shall reign forever;
 your God, O Zion, through all generations. R.

Second Reading *(James 5:7-10)*

Be patient, brothers and sisters, until the **coming of the Lord**. See how the farmer waits for the precious fruit of the earth, being patient with it until it receives the early and the late rains. You too must be patient. Make your hearts firm, because the coming of the Lord is at hand. Do not complain, brothers and sisters, about one another, that you may not be judged. Behold, the Judge is standing before the gates. Take as an example of hardship and patience, brothers and sisters, the prophets who spoke in the name of the Lord.

The word of the Lord. **Thanks be to God.**

Gospel *(Matthew 11:2-11)*

A reading from the holy Gospel according to Matthew.
Glory to you, O Lord.

When John the Baptist heard in prison of the works of the Christ, he sent his disciples to Jesus with this question, "Are you the one who is to come, or should we look for another?" Jesus said to them in reply, "Go and tell John what you hear and see: the blind regain their sight, the lame walk, lepers are cleansed, the deaf hear, the dead are raised, and the poor have the good news proclaimed to them. And blessed is the one who takes no offense at me."

As they were going off, Jesus began to speak to the crowds about John, "What did you go out to the desert to see? A **reed** swayed by the wind? Then what did you go out to see? Someone dressed in fine clothing? Those who wear fine clothing are in royal palaces. Then why did you go out? To see a **prophet**? Yes, I tell you, and more than a prophet. This is the one about whom it is written:

> Behold, I am sending my messenger ahead of you;
>   he will prepare your way before you.

Amen, I say to you, among those born of women there has been none greater than John the Baptist; yet the least in the kingdom of heaven is greater than he."

The Gospel of the Lord. **Praise to you, Lord Jesus Christ.**

Key Words

Lebanon is a country at the eastern end of the Mediterranean Sea, bordering on modern-day Israel.

Carmel refers to a coastal mountain in Israel. Mount Carmel marks the northern reach of the plain of **Sharon**, a flat region that includes the modern city of Tel Aviv.

If someone is **oppressed**, then they are being very badly treated by others. Oppression deadens the soul and must be opposed by working for peace and justice.

The **coming of the Lord** is a reference to the Second Coming of Jesus, at the end of time. The first Christians thought that Jesus would be returning in their own lifetime; they expected it to happen soon.

A **reed** is a thin shoot of a plant, often found near water. It is thin and flexible, and bends with the wind.

Prophets were holy men and women who spoke publicly against poverty and injustice, and criticized the people whenever they refused to listen to God's word. Many of the books of the Old Testament were written by prophets (Isaiah, Jeremiah, Amos, and Micah, for example).

DECEMBER 18
4th Sunday of Advent

First Reading (Isaiah 7:10-14)

The LORD spoke to **Ahaz**, saying: Ask for a sign from the LORD, your God; let it be deep as the netherworld, or high as the sky! But Ahaz answered, "I will not ask! I will not tempt the LORD!" Then Isaiah said: Listen, O **house of David**! Is it not enough for you to weary people, must you also weary my God? Therefore the Lord himself will give you this sign: the virgin shall conceive, and bear a son, and shall name him Emmanuel.

The word of the Lord. **Thanks be to God.**

Responsorial Psalm (Psalm 24:1-2, 3-4, 5-6)

R. **Let the Lord enter; he is king of glory.**

The LORD's are the earth and its fullness;
    the world and those who dwell in it.
For he founded it upon the seas
    and established it upon the rivers. R.
Who can ascend the mountain of the LORD?
    or who may stand in his holy place?
One whose hands are sinless, whose heart is clean,
    who desires not what is vain. R.
He shall receive a blessing from the LORD,
    a reward from God his savior.
Such is the race that seeks for him,
    that seeks the face of the God of Jacob. R.

Second Reading (Romans 1:1-7)

Paul, a slave of Christ Jesus, called to be an apostle and set apart for the **gospel** of God, which he promised previously through his prophets in the holy Scriptures, the gospel about his Son, descended from David according to the flesh, but established as Son of God in power according to the Spirit of holiness through resurrection from the dead, Jesus Christ our Lord. Through him we have received the grace of **apostleship**, to bring about the obedience of faith, for the sake of his name, among all the **Gentiles**, among whom are you also, who are called to belong to Jesus Christ; to all the beloved of God in

Rome, called to be holy. Grace to you and peace from God our Father and the Lord Jesus Christ.

The word of the Lord. **Thanks be to God.**

Gospel *(Matthew 1:18-24)*

A reading from the holy Gospel according to Matthew.
Glory to you, O Lord.

This is how the birth of Jesus Christ came about. When his mother Mary was **betrothed** to Joseph, but before they lived together, she was found with child through the Holy Spirit. Joseph her husband, since he was a righteous man, yet unwilling to expose her to shame, decided to divorce her quietly. Such was his intention when, behold, the angel of the Lord appeared to him in a dream and said, "Joseph, son of David, do not be afraid to take Mary your wife into your home. For it is through the Holy Spirit that this child has been conceived in her. She will bear a son and you are to name him Jesus, because he will save his people from their sins." All this took place to fulfill what the Lord had said through the prophet:

Behold, the virgin shall conceive and bear a son,
and they shall name him Emmanuel,

which means "God is with us." When Joseph awoke, he did as the angel of the Lord had commanded him and took his wife into his home.

The Gospel of the Lord. **Praise to you, Lord Jesus Christ.**

Key Words

Ahaz was a king of Israel who was not well thought of. He was not true to the people's covenant with God, he worshipped other gods that he himself had created, and he closed the temple.

When the prophet Isaiah speaks to the **house of David**, he is speaking to all the Israelites. This is one of the names by which all the people of Israel were known.

The Letter of Saint Paul to the Romans is the longest surviving letter that Saint Paul wrote. The Christians who lived in Rome belonged to a small community. Paul wanted to travel to preach in Spain and stop on the way in Rome to visit the Christians. He sent this letter ahead in order to encourage them and to remind them of the teachings of Jesus.

The word **gospel** means the whole message that Jesus brought us. It is a word meaning the "good news."

Apostleship is a mission that God gave to Saint Paul, to announce the good news of the resurrection of Jesus—that Jesus conquered death. This is also the mission of all Christians: we are all apostles through our baptism.

The **Gentiles** are people who are not Jewish. When Saint Paul speaks of Gentiles, he means Greeks and Romans living within the Roman Empire.

Saint **Matthew** was the author of one of the four gospels. Matthew's gospel tells us about the life of Jesus and emphasizes that he is the promised Messiah, and that the Church is now the Chosen People, the new Israel.

Joseph and Mary were **betrothed**, but they did not live together before marriage. For this reason, when Mary became pregnant, Joseph at first thought they shouldn't get married. But Joseph obeyed what the Lord told him in a dream, and he kept his promise to Mary and became Jesus' earthly father.

DECEMBER 25

Christmas
The Nativity of the Lord
(Mass During the Night)

First Reading *(Isaiah 9:1-6)*

The people who walked in darkness
    have seen a great light;
upon those who dwelt in the land of gloom
    a light has shone.
You have brought them abundant joy
    and great rejoicing,
as they rejoice before you as at the harvest,
    as people make merry when dividing spoils.
For the yoke that burdened them,
    the pole on their shoulder,
and the rod of their taskmaster
    you have smashed, as on the day of Midian.
For every boot that tramped in battle,
    every cloak rolled in blood,
    will be burned as fuel for flames.
For a child is born to us, a son is given us;
    upon his shoulder dominion rests.
They name him Wonder-Counselor, God-Hero,
    Father-Forever, Prince of Peace.
His dominion is vast
    and forever peaceful,
from David's throne, and over his kingdom,
    which he confirms and sustains
by judgment and justice,
    both now and forever.
The zeal of the Lord of hosts will do this!

The word of the Lord. **Thanks be to God.**

Responsorial Psalm *(Psalm 96: 1-2, 2-3, 11-12, 13)*

R. **Today is born our Savior, Christ the Lord.**

Sing to the LORD a new song;
    sing to the LORD, all you lands.
Sing to the LORD; bless his name. R.
Announce his salvation, day after day.
    Tell his glory among the nations;
    among all peoples, his wondrous deeds. R.

> Let the heavens be glad and the earth rejoice;
>> let the sea and what fills it resound;
>> let the plains be joyful and all that is in them!
> Then shall all the trees of the forest **exult**. R⁊
> They shall exult before the LORD, for he comes;
>> for he comes to rule the earth.
> He shall rule the world with justice
>> and the peoples with his constancy R⁊

Second Reading *(Titus 2:11-14)*

Beloved: The grace of God has appeared, saving all and training us to reject godless ways and worldly desires and to live temperately, justly, and devoutly in this age, as we await the blessed hope, the appearance of the glory of our great God and savior Jesus Christ, who gave himself for us to deliver us from all lawlessness and to cleanse for himself a people as his own, eager to do what is good.

The word of the Lord. **Thanks be to God.**

Gospel *(Luke 2:1-14)*

A reading from the holy Gospel according to Luke.
Glory to you, O Lord.

In those days a decree went out from Caesar Augustus that the whole world should be enrolled. This was the first enrollment, when Quirinius was governor of Syria. So all went to be enrolled, each to his own town. And Joseph too went up from Galilee from the town of Nazareth to Judea, to the city of David that is called Bethlehem, because he was of the house and family of David, to be enrolled with Mary, his betrothed, who was with child. While they were there, the time came for her to have her child, and she gave birth to her firstborn son. She wrapped him in swaddling clothes and laid him in a **manger**, because there was no room for them in the inn.

Now there were shepherds in that region living in the fields and keeping the night watch over their flock. The **angel of the Lord** appeared to them and the glory of the Lord shone around them, and they were struck with great fear. The angel said to them, "Do not be afraid; for behold, I proclaim to you good news of great joy that will be for all the people. For today in the city of David a savior has been born for you who is Christ and Lord. And this will be a sign for you: you will find an infant wrapped in swaddling clothes and lying in a manger." And suddenly there was a multitude of the heavenly host with the angel, praising God and saying:

"Glory to God in the highest
   and on earth peace to those on whom his favor rests."

The Gospel of the Lord. **Praise to you, Lord Jesus Christ.**

Merry Christmas!

GLORY TO GOD
IN THE HIGHEST
AND ON EARTH PEACE
TO ALL PEOPLE!

Christmas Day is celebrated on December 25th, but the Christmas season lasts for just over two weeks this year, ending with the Baptism of Jesus in January. The liturgical color for this season is white, the color of joy and celebration.

Prophets like **Isaiah** were good men and women who spoke for God. Sometimes their messages were demanding: they asked people to change their lives and attitudes to grow closer to God. At other times, they brought words of comfort.

We **exult,** or show our joy, because our hearts are full of happiness: God has come to be with his people. In today's Psalm, we see that all creation—even the trees!—rejoice and glory in the Lord.

A **manger** is a wooden crate filled with hay to feed the animals in a stable. It comes from the French word *manger*, to eat. The baby Jesus was placed in a manger soon after he was born. It is amazing that God would choose to be born in such a simple place.

An **angel of the Lord** is a messenger of God. Angels appear many times in the Bible, as we see angels revealing God's plan in the lives of Jesus, Mary, and Joseph.

JANUARY 1

Solemnity of Mary,
the Holy Mother of God

First Reading *(Numbers 6:22-27)*

The LORD said to **Moses**: "Speak to **Aaron** and his sons and tell them: This is how you shall bless the Israelites. Say to them:
The LORD bless you and keep you!
The LORD let his face shine upon you, and be gracious to you!
The LORD look upon you kindly and give you peace!
So shall they invoke my name upon the Israelites,
and I will bless them."

The word of the Lord. **Thanks be to God.**

Responsorial Psalm *(Psalm 67:2-3, 5, 6, 8)*

R. May God bless us in his mercy.

May God have pity on us and bless us;
    may he let his face shine upon us.
So may your way be known upon earth;
    among all nations, your salvation. R.
May the nations be glad and exult
    because you rule the peoples in **equity**;
    the nations on the earth you guide. R.
May the peoples praise you, O God;
    may all the peoples praise you!
May God bless us,
    and may all the ends of the earth fear him! R.

Second Reading *(Galatians 4:4-7)*

Brothers and sisters: When the **fullness of time** had come, God sent his Son, born of a woman, born under the law, to ransom those under the law, so that we might receive adoption as sons. As proof that you are sons, God sent the Spirit of his Son into our hearts, crying out, "**Abba**, Father!" So you are no longer a slave but a son, and if a son then also an heir, through God.

The word of the Lord. **Thanks be to God.**

Gospel *(Luke 2:16-21)*

A reading from the holy Gospel according to Luke.
Glory to you, O Lord.

The shepherds went in haste to Bethlehem and found Mary and Joseph, and the infant lying in the manger. When they saw this, they made known the message that had been told them about this child. All who heard it were amazed by what had been told them by the shepherds. And Mary kept all these things, **reflecting** on them in her heart. Then the shepherds returned, glorifying and praising God for all they had heard and seen, just as it had been told to them.

When eight days were completed for his circumcision, he was named Jesus, the name given him by the angel before he was conceived in the womb.

The Gospel of the Lord.
Praise to you, Lord Jesus Christ.

Key Words

The **book of Numbers** is part of the Bible. It is called Numbers because it talks about many numbers and times when the people of Israel were counted. In Hebrew, it is called "In the Desert," because it tells of the travels of the Israelites in the desert after they left slavery in Egypt.

Moses was a friend of God who was born in Egypt when the Israelites were slaves there. When God asked him to lead the people to freedom, Moses said yes because he loved God and didn't want the people to suffer any more. The people left Egypt on a journey called the Exodus, about 1,250 years before the time of Jesus.

Aaron, Moses' older brother, helped him free the Israelites. When Moses went up Mount Sinai to receive God's law, Aaron stayed with the people.

To judge with **equity** is to be fair to everyone. In the Psalm, the psalmist is praising God for God's fairness to all people on earth.

Fullness of time means when the time was right for God to send Jesus into the world.

In Aramaic, the language Jesus spoke, **Abba** means "Daddy." By calling God "Abba," Jesus shows that we can talk to God with the same trust and love that small children have for their father.

Reflecting means to think about something a lot. Like all mothers, Mary remembered all the details surrounding the birth of her child, and recalled these memories over and over.

JANUARY 8
Epiphany of the Lord

First Reading *(Isaiah 60:1-6)*

Rise up in splendor, Jerusalem! Your light has come,
the glory of the LORD shines upon you.
See, darkness covers the earth,
and thick clouds cover the peoples;
but upon you the LORD shines,
and over you appears his glory.
Nations shall walk by your light,
and kings by your shining radiance.
Raise your eyes and look about;
they all gather and come to you:
your sons come from afar,
and your daughters in the arms of their nurses.

Then you shall be radiant at what you see,
your heart shall throb and overflow,
for the riches of the sea shall be emptied out before you,
the wealth of nations shall be brought to you.
Caravans of camels shall fill you,
dromedaries from **Midian** and **Ephah**;
all from **Sheba** shall come
bearing gold and frankincense,
and proclaiming the praises of the LORD.

The word of the Lord. **Thanks be to God.**

Responsorial Psalm *(Psalm 72:1-2, 7-8, 10-11, 12-13)*

R. **Lord, every nation on earth will adore you.**

O God, with your judgment endow the king,
and with your justice, the king's son;
he shall govern your people with justice
and your afflicted ones with judgment. R.
Justice shall flower in his days,
and profound peace, till the moon be no more.
May he rule from sea to sea,
and from the River to the ends of the earth. R.

R̶. **Lord, every nation on earth will adore you.**

The kings of Tarshish and the Isles shall offer gifts;
  the kings of Arabia and Seba shall bring tribute.
All kings shall pay him homage,
  all nations shall serve him. R̶.
For he shall rescue the poor when he cries out,
  and the afflicted when he has no one to help him.
He shall have pity for the lowly and the poor;
  the lives of the poor he shall save. R̶.

Second Reading *(Ephesians 3:2-3a, 5-6)*

Brothers and sisters: You have heard of the stewardship of God's grace that was given to me for your benefit, namely, that the **mystery** was made known to me by **revelation**. It was not made known to people in other generations as it has now been revealed to his holy apostles and prophets by the Spirit: that the Gentiles are coheirs, members of the same body, and copartners in the promise in Christ Jesus through the gospel.

The word of the Lord. **Thanks be to God.**

Gospel *(Matthew 2:1-12)*

A reading from the holy Gospel according to Matthew.
Glory to you, O Lord.

When Jesus was born in **Bethlehem of Judea**, in the days of King Herod, behold, magi from the east arrived in Jerusalem, saying, "Where is the newborn king of the Jews? We saw his star at its rising and have come to do him **homage**." When King Herod heard this, he was greatly troubled, and all Jerusalem with him. Assembling all the chief priests and the scribes of the people, he inquired of them where the Christ was to be born. They said to him, "In Bethlehem of Judea, for thus it has been written through the prophet:
  And you, Bethlehem, land of Judah,
    are by no means least among the rulers of Judah;
  since from you shall come a ruler,
    who is to shepherd my people Israel."

Then Herod called the magi secretly and ascertained from them the time of the star's appearance. He sent them to Bethlehem and said, "Go and search diligently for the child. When you have found him, bring me word, that I too may go and do him homage." After their audience with the king they set out. And behold, the star that they had seen at its rising preceded them, until it came and stopped over the place where the child was. They were overjoyed at seeing the star, and on entering the house they saw the child with Mary his mother. They prostrated themselves and did him homage. Then they opened their treasures and offered him gifts of **gold, frankincense, and myrrh**. And having been warned in a dream not to return to Herod, they departed for their country by another way.

The Gospel of the Lord. **Praise to you, Lord Jesus Christ.**

Key Words

Epiphany is a Greek word that means "unveiling" or "revelation." God revealed his love for all people by sending us his Son, Jesus, as a human being—as a baby.

Midian, Ephah, and Sheba were three ancient kingdoms near Israel. In the book of the prophet Isaiah in the Bible, they represent all the nations outside Israel.

The **Ephesians** were a group of Christians in the city of Ephesus. A letter Saint Paul wrote to them is now part of the Bible. Ephesus is located in modern-day Turkey.

A **mystery** is something that is very hard to understand. In Saint Paul's letter to the Ephesians, the mystery Paul speaks of is God's plan to create a human community in Christ.

To know something by **revelation** means that God has shown or given someone this knowledge. It is not known by human means.

Bethlehem of Judea is the city of King David, one of Jesus' ancestors. Joseph and Mary went to Bethlehem for a census (an official counting of all the people). Jesus was born during their stay there.

To pay someone **homage** is to show your respect or honor for them in a public way, such as by bowing or bringing gifts.

Gold, frankincense, and myrrh were three very expensive gifts: gold is a precious metal; frankincense and myrrh are rare, sweet-smelling incenses.

First Reading *(Isaiah 49:3, 5-6)*

The LORD said to me: You are my servant,
Israel, through whom I show my glory.
Now the LORD has spoken
who formed me as his **servant** from the womb,
that **Jacob** may be brought back to him
and Israel gathered to him;
and I am made glorious in the sight of the LORD,
and my God is now my strength!
It is too little, the LORD says, for you to be my servant,
to raise up the tribes of Jacob,
and restore the survivors of Israel;
I will make you a light to the nations,
that my salvation may reach to the ends of the earth.

The word of the Lord. **Thanks be to God.**

Responsorial Psalm *(Psalm 40:2, 4, 7-8, 8-9, 10)*

R. **Here am I, Lord; I come to do your will.**

I have waited, waited for the LORD,
and he stooped toward me and heard my cry.
And he put a new song into my mouth,
a hymn to our God. R.
Sacrifice or offering you wished not,
but ears open to obedience you gave me.
Holocausts or sin-offerings you sought not;
then said I, "Behold I come." R.
"In the written scroll it is prescribed for me,
to do your will, O my God, is my delight,
and your law is within my heart!" R.
I announced your justice in the vast assembly;
I did not restrain my lips, as you, O LORD, know. R.

Second Reading *(1 Corinthians 1:1-3)*

Paul, called to be an apostle of Christ Jesus by the will of God, and **Sosthenes** our brother, to the church of God that is in Corinth, to you who have been sanctified in Christ Jesus, called to be holy, with all those everywhere who call upon the name of our Lord Jesus Christ, their Lord and ours. **Grace to you and peace** from God our Father and the Lord Jesus Christ.

The word of the Lord. **Thanks be to God.**

Gospel *(John 1:29-34)*

A reading from the holy Gospel according to John.
Glory to you, O Lord.

John the Baptist saw Jesus coming toward him and said, "Behold, the **Lamb of God**, who takes away the sin of the world. He is the one of whom I said, 'A man is coming after me who ranks ahead of me because he existed before me.' I did not know him, but the reason why I came baptizing with water was that he might be made known to Israel." John **testified** further, saying, "I saw the Spirit come down like a dove from heaven and remain upon him. I did not know him, but the one who sent me to baptize with water told me, 'On whomever you see the Spirit come down and remain, he is the one who will baptize with the Holy Spirit.' Now I have seen and testified that he is the **Son of God**."

The Gospel of the Lord. **Praise to you, Lord Jesus Christ.**

Key Words

A **servant** is someone who carries out the wishes of their master. God's servant will bring together the tribes of Israel. Christians believe that Jesus, the Messiah, came to bring all people to God.

Jacob was the grandson of Abraham and the father of many children. His children were the first people in the twelve tribes of the Jewish people. In this reading, Jacob represents all the people of Israel.

Sosthenes was a friend and companion of Saint Paul who helped him spread the good news of Jesus Christ to the people in Corinth in Greece.

When Saint Paul wishes "**grace to you and peace**," he is expressing his wish that we will all live according to the gifts that Jesus' salvation brings, especially peace.

The **Lamb of God** is Jesus. Jewish people made sacrifices of animals to God. Because Saint John the Baptist himself knew the cost of announcing the love of God, he could see that Jesus would be the Lamb of God.

To **testify** is to announce a truth with words or deeds, so that others will know the truth. We testify that Jesus lives when we live as he taught us.

Saint John the Baptist calls Jesus the **Son of God**, showing that Jesus is the Messiah, the long-awaited one sent from God to bring us salvation.

JANUARY 22

3rd Sunday in Ordinary Time

First Reading (*Isaiah 8:23–9:3*)

First the Lord degraded the land of **Zebulun** and the land of
Naphtali; but in the end he has glorified the seaward road, the
land west of the Jordan, the District of the Gentiles.
Anguish has taken wing, dispelled is darkness:
for there is no gloom where but now there was distress.
The people who **walked in darkness**
have seen a great light;
upon those who dwelt in the land of gloom
a light has shone.
You have brought them abundant joy
and great rejoicing,
as they rejoice before you as at the harvest,
as people make merry when dividing spoils.
For the yoke that burdened them,
the pole on their shoulder,
and the rod of their taskmaster
you have smashed, as on the day of Midian.

The word of the Lord. **Thanks be to God.**

Responsorial Psalm (*Psalm 27:1, 4, 13-14*)

R. **The Lord is my light and my salvation.**

The Lord is my light and my salvation;
whom should I fear?
The Lord is my life's refuge;
of whom should I be afraid? R.
One thing I ask of the Lord;
this I seek:
To dwell in the house of the Lord
all the days of my life,
that I may gaze on the loveliness of the Lord
and contemplate his temple. R.
I believe that I shall see the bounty of the Lord
in the land of the living.
Wait for the Lord with courage;
be stouthearted, and wait for the Lord. R.

Second Reading *(1 Corinthians 1:10-13, 17)*

I urge you, brothers and sisters, in the name of our Lord Jesus Christ, that all of you agree in what you say, and that there be no divisions among you, but that you be united in the same mind and in the same purpose. For it has been reported to me about you, my brothers and sisters, by Chloe's people, that there are rivalries among you. I mean that each of you is saying, "I belong to Paul," or "I belong to Apollos," or "I belong to Cephas," or "I belong to Christ." Is Christ divided? Was Paul crucified for you? Or were you baptized in the name of Paul? For Christ did not send me to baptize but to preach the gospel, and not with the wisdom of human eloquence, so that the cross of Christ might not be emptied of its meaning.

The word of the Lord. **Thanks be to God.**

Gospel *(Matthew 4:12-23)*

The shorter version ends at the asterisks.

A reading from the holy Gospel according to Matthew.
Glory to you, O Lord.

When Jesus heard that John had been arrested, he withdrew to Galilee. He left Nazareth and went to live in Capernaum by the sea, in the region of Zebulun and Naphtali, that what had been said through Isaiah the prophet might be fulfilled:
> Land of Zebulun and land of Naphtali,
>> the way to the sea, beyond the Jordan,
>> Galilee of the Gentiles,
> the people who sit in darkness have seen a great light,
> on those dwelling in a land overshadowed by death
>> light has arisen.

From that time on, Jesus began to preach and say, "**Repent**, for the **kingdom of heaven** is at hand."

* * *

As he was walking by the Sea of Galilee, he saw two brothers, Simon who is called Peter, and his brother Andrew, casting a net into the sea; they were fishermen. He said to them, "Come after me, and I will make you fishers of men." At once they left their nets and followed him. He walked along from there and saw two other brothers, James, the son of Zebedee, and his brother John. They were in a boat, with their father Zebedee, mending their nets. He called them, and immediately they left their boat and their father and followed him. He went around all of Galilee, teaching in their synagogues, proclaiming the gospel of the kingdom, and curing every disease and illness among the people.

The Gospel of the Lord. **Praise to you, Lord Jesus Christ.**

Key Words

and the experience changed his whole life. When he was baptized he changed his name to **Paul** and became a great apostle, traveling to cities all around the Mediterranean Sea to tell people about the love of Jesus. Several letters he wrote are now in the Bible.

When Isaiah mentions **Zebulun** and **Naphtali**, his listeners remember towns where God had shown his anger because the people did not heed his words. God promises to send the Messiah who will bring freedom and joy to God's people.

People, families, or even nations can **walk in darkness** when they feel lost and do not know where to turn. They need God's light to show them the way.

Saul was a man who bullied and terrorized the first Christians. One day, he had a vision of the risen Jesus

The holy Gospel according to Matthew is the first book in the New Testament. This gospel tells us about the life of Jesus. It points out that he is the promised Messiah, and that the Church is the chosen people, the new Israel.

To **repent** means to be sorry for doing something wrong, and to change your way of thinking and living for the better.

In the **kingdom of heaven**, all people will be brought together in God. We will all live like brothers and sisters, sharing in God's abundant love and mercy.

JANUARY 29

4th Sunday in Ordinary Time

First Reading *(Zephaniah 2:3; 3:12-13)*

Seek the LORD, all you humble of the earth,
who have observed his law;
seek justice, seek **humility**;
perhaps you may be sheltered
on the day of the LORD's anger.

But I will leave as a remnant in your midst
a people humble and lowly,
who shall take refuge in the name of the LORD:
the **remnant of Israel**.
They shall do no wrong
and speak no lies;
nor shall there be found in their mouths
a deceitful tongue;
they shall pasture and couch their flocks
with none to disturb them.

The word of the Lord. **Thanks be to God.**

Responsorial Psalm *(Psalm 146:6-7, 8-9, 9-10)*

R. **Blessed are the poor in spirit; the kingdom
of heaven is theirs!** *Or* **Alleluia.**

The LORD keeps faith forever,
secures justice for the oppressed,
gives food to the hungry.
The LORD sets captives free. R.
The LORD gives sight to the blind;
the Lord raises up those who were bowed down.
The LORD loves the just;
the LORD protects strangers. R.
The fatherless and the widow he sustains,
but the way of the wicked he thwarts.
The LORD shall reign forever;
your God, O Zion, through all generations. Alleluia. R.

Second Reading *(1 Corinthians 1:26-31)*

Consider your own calling, brothers and sisters. Not many of you were wise by human standards, not many were powerful, not many were of noble birth. Rather, God chose the foolish of the world to shame the wise, and God chose the weak of the world to shame the strong, and God chose the lowly and despised of the world, those who count for nothing, to reduce to nothing those who are something, so that no human being might boast before God. It is due to him that you are in Christ Jesus, who became for us wisdom from God, as well as righteousness, sanctification, and redemption, so that, as it is written, "Whoever boasts, should boast in the Lord."

The word of the Lord. **Thanks be to God.**

Gospel *(Matthew 5:1-12a)*

A reading from the holy Gospel according to Matthew.
Glory to you, O Lord.

When Jesus saw the crowds, he went up the mountain, and after he had sat down, his disciples came to him. He began to teach them, saying:
"Blessed are the **poor in spirit**,
for theirs is the kingdom of heaven.
Blessed are they who mourn,
for they will be comforted.
Blessed are the meek,
for they will inherit the land.
Blessed are they who hunger and thirst for righteousness,
for they will be satisfied.
Blessed are the **merciful**,
for they will be shown mercy.
Blessed are the clean of heart,
for they will see God.
Blessed are the peacemakers,
for they will be called children of God.
Blessed are they who are persecuted for the sake of righteousness,
for theirs is the kingdom of heaven.
Blessed are you when they insult you and persecute you
and utter every kind of evil against you falsely because of me.
Rejoice and be glad,
for your reward will be great in heaven."

The Gospel of the Lord. **Praise to you, Lord Jesus Christ.**

Key Words

The prophet **Zephaniah** lived about 700 years before Jesus was born. The people of Israel had fallen away from their faith. Zephaniah tried to help them return to God.

People who have **humility** do not show off or boast. They don't worry about how much money they have, but try in their hearts to do the will of God and think of others before they think of themselves.

In times when many of the Israelites had turned away from God, the few who remained faithful to God's covenant were call the **remnant of Israel**.

The **Corinthians** were a community of Christians who lived in Corinth, a city in Greece. Saint Paul wrote them several letters, two of which were preserved and are in the Bible.

The **poor in spirit** are people who put their confidence in God and do not worry about material things. The poor in spirit are in fact rich in God's Spirit.

Those who are **merciful** share in God's loving concern for everyone, but most especially for the poor and the weak. They are always ready to forgive and show mercy. Jesus asks us to be merciful.

First Reading *(Isaiah 58:7-10)*

Thus says the LORD:
  Share your bread with the hungry,
    shelter the oppressed and the homeless;
  clothe the naked when you see them,
    and do not turn your back on your own.
  Then your light shall break forth like the dawn,
    and your wound shall quickly be healed;
  your **vindication** shall go before you,
    and the glory of the LORD shall be your rear guard.
  Then you shall call, and the LORD will answer,
    you shall cry for help, and he will say: Here I am!
  If you remove from your midst
    oppression, false accusation and malicious speech;
  if you bestow your bread on the hungry
    and satisfy the afflicted;
  then light shall rise for you in the darkness
    and the gloom shall become for you like midday.

The word of the Lord. **Thanks be to God.**

Responsorial Psalm *(Psalm 112:4-5, 6-7, 8-9)*

R. **The just man is a light in darkness to the upright.**
  Or **Alleluia.**

Light shines through the darkness for the upright;
  he is gracious and merciful and just.
Well for the man who is gracious and lends,
  who conducts his affairs with justice. R.
He shall never be moved;
  the just one shall be in everlasting remembrance.
An evil report he shall not fear;
  his heart is firm, trusting in the LORD. R.
His heart is steadfast; he shall not fear.
  Lavishly he gives to the poor;
His justice shall endure forever;
  his horn shall be exalted in glory. R.

Second Reading *(1 Corinthians 2:1-5)*

When I came to you, brothers and sisters, proclaiming the mystery of God, I did not come with **sublimity of words** or of wisdom. For I resolved to know nothing while I was with you except Jesus Christ, and him crucified. I came to you in weakness and fear and much trembling, and my message and my proclamation were not with persuasive words of wisdom, but with a demonstration of Spirit and power, so that your faith might rest not on human wisdom but on the power of God.

The word of the Lord. **Thanks be to God.**

Gospel *(Matthew 5:13-16)*

A reading from the holy Gospel according to Matthew.
Glory to you, O Lord.

Jesus said to his disciples: "You are the **salt** of the earth. But if salt loses its taste, with what can it be seasoned? It is no longer good for anything but to be thrown out and trampled underfoot. You are the light of the world. A city set on a mountain cannot be hidden. Nor do they light a lamp and then put it under a bushel basket; it is set on a lampstand, where it gives light to all in the house. Just so, your light must shine before others, that they may see your good deeds and glorify your heavenly Father."

The Gospel of the Lord. **Praise to you, Lord Jesus Christ.**

Key Words

Vindication is when a person proves that something is true or right. When we obey God and defend what is right, God is our vindicator; God shows that our work is good and right.

....

Saint Paul tells the people of Corinth that our lives are not based on "**sublimity of words**," meaning grand or impressive words of wisdom. Instead, he says our lives are based on the work of the Spirit. We do not rely on our own power but on the power of God.

Salt brings out the flavors of the foods we eat. In ancient times, salt was an essential preservative for meat, fish, and vegetables, since refrigerators did not exist. Because of its long-lasting, preserving nature, salt became a symbol of enduring friendships and a sign of a contract between persons or groups. As "salt of the earth," Jesus' followers bring out the best flavors in life, preserve the good news of Jesus' loving presence, and are faithful friends of God.

First Reading *(Sirach 15:15-20)*

If you choose you can keep the commandments,
　　they will save you;
　　if you trust in God, you too shall live;
he has set before you fire and water;
　　to whichever you choose, stretch forth your hand.
Before man are life and death, good and evil,
　　whichever he chooses shall be given him.
Immense is the wisdom of the Lord;
　　he is mighty in power, and all-seeing.
The eyes of God are on those who fear him;
　　he understands man's every deed.
No one does he command to act unjustly,
　　to none does he give license to sin.

The word of the Lord. **Thanks be to God.**

Responsorial Psalm *(Psalm 119:1-2, 4-5, 17-18, 33-34)*

R. **Blessed are they who follow the law of the Lord!**

Blessed are they whose way is blameless,
　　who walk in the **law** of the Lord.
Blessed are they who observe his **decrees**,
　　who seek him with all their heart. R.
You have commanded that your precepts
　　be diligently kept.
Oh, that I might be firm in the ways
　　of keeping your **statutes**! R.
Be good to your servant, that I may live
　　and keep your words.
Open my eyes, that I may consider
　　the wonders of your law. R.
Instruct me, O Lord, in the way of your statutes,
　　that I may exactly observe them.
Give me discernment, that I may observe your law
　　and keep it with all my heart. R.

Second Reading *(1 Corinthians 2:6-10)*

Brothers and sisters: We speak a wisdom to those who are mature, not a wisdom of this age, nor of the rulers of this age who are passing away. Rather, we speak God's wisdom, **mysterious, hidden**, which God predetermined before the ages for our glory, and which none of the rulers of this age knew; for, if they had known it, they would not have crucified the Lord of glory. But as it is written:

What eye has not seen, and ear has not heard,
and what has not entered the human heart,
what God has prepared for those who love him,
this God has revealed to us through the Spirit.
For the Spirit scrutinizes everything, even the depths of God.

The word of the Lord. **Thanks be to God.**

Gospel *(Matthew 5:17-37)*

For the shorter version, omit the indented parts in brackets.

A reading from the holy Gospel according to Matthew.
Glory to you, O Lord.

Jesus said to his disciples:
["Do not think that I have come to abolish the law or the prophets. I have come not to abolish but to **fulfill**. Amen, I say to you, until heaven and earth pass away, not the smallest letter or the smallest part of a letter will pass from the law, until all things have taken place. Therefore, whoever breaks one of the least of these commandments and teaches others to do so will be called least in the kingdom of heaven. But whoever obeys and teaches these commandments will be called greatest in the kingdom of heaven.]
I tell you, unless your righteousness surpasses that of the scribes and Pharisees, you will not enter the kingdom of heaven.

"You have heard that it was said to your ancestors, *You shall not kill; and whoever kills will be liable to judgment.* But I say to you, whoever is angry with his brother will be liable to judgment.
[and whoever says to his brother, 'Raqa,' will be answerable to the Sanhedrin; and whoever says, 'You fool,' will be liable to fiery Gehenna. Therefore, if you bring your gift to the altar, and there recall that your brother has anything

against you, leave your gift there at the altar, go first and be reconciled with your brother, and then come and offer your gift. Settle with your opponent quickly while on the way to court. Otherwise your opponent will hand you over to the judge, and the judge will hand you over to the guard, and you will be thrown into prison. Amen, I say to you, you will not be released until you have paid the last penny.]

"You have heard that it was said, *You shall not commit adultery*. But I say to you, everyone who looks at a woman with lust has already committed adultery with her in his heart.

[If your right eye causes you to sin, tear it out and throw it away. It is better for you to lose one of your members than to have your whole body thrown into Gehenna. And if your right hand causes you to sin, cut it off and throw it away. It is better for you to lose one of your members than to have your whole body go into Gehenna.

"It was also said, *Whoever divorces his wife must give her a bill of divorce*. But I say to you, whoever divorces his wife—unless the marriage is unlawful—causes her to commit adultery, and whoever marries a divorced woman commits adultery.]

"Again you have heard that it was said to your ancestors, *Do not* **take a false oath,** *but make good to the Lord all that you vow*. But I say to you, do not swear at all;

[not by heaven, for it is God's throne; nor by the earth, for it is his footstool; nor by Jerusalem, for it is the city of the great King. Do not swear by your head, for you cannot make a single hair white or black.]

Let your 'Yes' mean 'Yes,' and your 'No' mean 'No.' Anything more is from the evil one."

The Gospel of the Lord. **Praise to you, Lord Jesus Christ.**

Key Words

The book of **Sirach** in the Bible was written 200 years before Jesus was born. In some Bibles, it is called the book of Ecclesiasticus. It tells us that wisdom is respecting God and obeying God's plans for us.

In the Psalm, the writer uses legal terms when he speaks about following God: **law, decrees, precepts and statutes**. We might think it is hard to follow all these rules, but the psalmist sees these laws as blessings and life-giving. Jesus says in the Gospel that he has come not to abolish the law but to **fulfill** it.

Saint Paul speaks of God's wisdom as **mysterious and hidden**: it cannot be known by logic or reason. God reveals his wisdom to us through the Spirit. Those who rely on worldly wisdom instead will not have eternal life.

To swear is to make a promise relying on something or someone else, and to **take a false oath** is to break a promise, or to lie when we are making that promise. Because we are not perfect as God is, Jesus says that it is better if we do not make any promises that we cannot keep.

First Reading *(Leviticus 19:1-2, 17-18)*

The LORD said to Moses, "Speak to the whole Israelite community and tell them: Be holy, for I, the LORD, your God, am holy.

"You shall not bear hatred for your brother or sister in your heart. Though you may have to **reprove** your fellow citizen, do not incur sin because of him. Take no revenge and cherish no grudge against any of your people. You shall love your neighbor as yourself. I am the LORD."

The word of the Lord. **Thanks be to God.**

Responsorial Psalm *(Psalm 103:1-2, 3-4, 8, 10, 12-13)*

R. **The Lord is kind and merciful.**

Bless the LORD, O my soul;
    and all my being, bless his holy name.
Bless the LORD, O my soul,
    and forget not all his benefits. R.
He pardons all your iniquities,
    heals all your ills.
He redeems your life from destruction,
    crowns you with kindness and compassion. R.
Merciful and gracious is the LORD,
    slow to anger and abounding in kindness.
Not according to our sins does he deal with us,
    nor does he requite us according to our crimes. R.
As far as the east is from the west,
    so far has he put our transgressions from us.
As a father has compassion on his children,
    so the LORD has compassion on those
      who fear him. R.

Second Reading *(1 Corinthians 3:16-23)*

Brothers and sisters: Do you not know that you are the **temple** of God, and that the Spirit of God dwells in you? If anyone destroys God's temple, God will destroy that person; for the temple of God, which you are, is holy.

Let no one deceive himself. If any one among you considers himself wise in this age, let him become a fool, so as to become wise. For the wisdom of this world is foolishness in the eyes of God, for it is written:

God catches the wise in their own ruses,

and again:

The Lord knows the thoughts of the wise,
that they are vain.

So let no one boast about human beings, for everything belongs to you, Paul or Apollos or Cephas, or the world or life or death, or the present or the future: all belong to you, and you to Christ, and Christ to God.

The word of the Lord. **Thanks be to God.**

Gospel *(Matthew 5:38-48)*

A reading from the holy Gospel according to Matthew.
Glory to you, O Lord.

Jesus said to his disciples: "You have heard that it was said, **An eye for an eye** *and a tooth for a tooth.* But I say to you, offer no resistance to one who is evil. When someone strikes you on your right cheek, turn the other one as well. If anyone wants to go to law with you over your **tunic**, hand over your **cloak** as well. Should anyone press you into service for one mile, go for two miles. Give to the one who asks of you, and do not turn your back on one who wants to borrow.

"You have heard that it was said, *You shall love your neighbor and hate your enemy.* But I say to you, love your enemies and pray for those who persecute you, that you may be children of your heavenly Father, for he makes his sun rise on the bad and the good, and causes rain to fall on the just and the unjust. For if you love those who love you, what recompense will you have? Do not the tax collectors do the same? And if you greet your brothers only, what is unusual about that? Do not the pagans do the same? So be perfect, just as your heavenly Father is perfect."

The Gospel of the Lord. **Praise to you, Lord Jesus Christ.**

To **reprove** is to correct someone or show them where they have done something wrong. The Lord tells Moses that we have a duty to do this, but we must do it in a loving way—loving our neighbor as ourselves.

The **temple** in Jerusalem was the place on earth where God's Spirit was seen to dwell. It is startling when Saint Paul reminds us that our bodies and souls are God's temple! We must take good care of our bodies as well as live lives of justice and mercy.

It seems harsh to us when Jesus mentions the saying, "**An eye for an eye**." But this saying was seen as just and fair, for it meant that compensation for an injury was limited to the value of what had been harmed or taken. What Jesus proposes is radical and surprising, going beyond what was ordinarily seen as acceptable.

In the time of Jesus, most people owned two garments—a **tunic** for daytime use, and a **cloak** to provide warmth night and day. When Jesus says to offer not only your shirt but your cloak as well, he is saying to let go of everything you have!

FEBRUARY 26
8th Sunday in Ordinary Time

First Reading *(Isaiah 49:14-15)*

Zion said, "The LORD has forsaken me;
   my Lord has forgotten me."
Can a mother forget her infant,
   be without tenderness for the child of her womb?
Even should she forget,
   I will never forget you.

The word of the Lord. **Thanks be to God.**

Responsorial Psalm *(Psalm 62:2-3, 6-7, 8-9)*

R. **Rest in God alone, my soul.**

Only in God is my soul at rest;
   from him comes my salvation.
He only is my rock and my salvation,
   my stronghold; I shall not be disturbed at all. R.
Only in God be at rest, my soul,
   for from him comes my hope.
He only is my rock and my salvation,
   my stronghold; I shall not be disturbed. R.
With God is my safety and my glory,
   he is the rock of my strength; my refuge is in God.
Trust in him at all times, O my people!
   Pour out your hearts before him. R.

Second Reading *(1 Corinthians 4:1-5)*

Brothers and sisters: Thus should one regard us: as servants of Christ and **stewards** of the mysteries of God. Now it is of course required of stewards that they be found trustworthy. It does not concern me in the least that I be judged by you or any human tribunal; I do not even pass judgment on myself; I am not conscious of anything against me, but I do not thereby stand acquitted; the one who judges me is the Lord. Therefore do not make any judgment before the appointed time, until the Lord comes, for he will bring to light what is hidden in darkness and will manifest the motives of our hearts, and then everyone will receive praise from God.

The word of the Lord. **Thanks be to God.**

Gospel *(Matthew 6:24-34)*

A reading from the holy Gospel according to Matthew.
Glory to you, O Lord.

Jesus said to his disciples: "No one can serve two masters. He will either hate one and love the other, or be devoted to one and despise the other. You cannot serve God and mammon.

"Therefore I tell you, do not worry about your life, what you will eat or drink, or about your body, what you will wear. Is not life more than food and the body more than clothing? Look at the birds in the sky; they do not sow or reap, they gather nothing into barns, yet your heavenly Father feeds them. Are not you more important than they? Can any of you by worrying add a single moment to your life-span? Why are you anxious about clothes? Learn from the way the wild flowers grow. They do not work or spin. But I tell you that not even **Solomon** in all his splendor was clothed like one of them. If God so clothes the grass of the field, which **grows today** and is thrown into the oven tomorrow, will he not much more provide for you, O you of little faith? So do not worry and say, 'What are we to eat?' or 'What are we to drink?' or 'What are we to wear?' All these things the pagans seek. Your heavenly Father knows that you need them all. But seek first the kingdom of God and his righteousness, and all these things will be given you besides. Do not worry about tomorrow; tomorrow will take care of itself. Sufficient for a day is its own evil."

The Gospel of the Lord. **Praise to you, Lord Jesus Christ.**

Key Words

Zion was the name of a hill in Jerusalem, where the temple was built, but the city and the people living within it were often called Zion as well. Zion is another way of naming the entire nation, the whole people of God.

Stewards are people who are given the responsibility to care for and manage things that belong to someone else. They are given this task because they are honest and trustworthy. Saint Paul tells us that as Christians we are stewards of God's mysteries.

Solomon became king of Israel after his father David. Solomon was famous for his wisdom and for the beauty and magnificence of his royal court.

The land around Israel is naturally dry and brown most of the year. When wild grasses and flowers bloom, they live a short time and then wither—they **grow today** and are gone shortly after. Jesus uses the example of these plants to show us how insignificant are the things we worry so much about.

MARCH 1
Ash Wednesday

First Reading *(Joel 2:12-18)*

Even now, says the Lord,
    return to me with your whole heart,
    with fasting, and weeping, and mourning;
Rend your hearts, not your garments,
    and return to the Lord, your God.
For gracious and merciful is he,
    slow to anger, rich in kindness,
    and relenting in punishment.
Perhaps he will again relent
    and leave behind him a blessing,
Offerings and libations
    for the Lord, your God.

Blow the trumpet in Zion!
    proclaim a fast,
    call an assembly;
Gather the people,
    notify the **congregation**;
Assemble the elders,
    gather the children
    and the infants at the breast;
Let the bridegroom quit his room
    and the bride her chamber.
Between the porch and the altar
    let the priests, the ministers of the Lord, weep,
And say, "Spare, O Lord, your people,
    and make not your heritage a reproach,
    with the nations ruling over them!
Why should they say among the peoples,
    'Where is their God?' "

Then the Lord was stirred to concern for his land
    and took pity on his people.

The word of the Lord. **Thanks be to God.**

Responsorial Psalm
(Psalm 51:3-4, 5-6ab, 12-13, 14 and 17)

R. **Be merciful, O Lord, for we have sinned.**

Have mercy on me, O God, in your goodness;
    in the greatness of your compassion
        wipe out my offense.
Thoroughly wash me from my guilt
    and of my sin cleanse me. R.
For I acknowledge my offense,
    and my sin is before me always:
"Against you only have I sinned,
    and done what is evil in your sight." R.
A clean heart create for me, O God,
    and a steadfast spirit renew within me.
Cast me not out from your presence,
    and your Holy Spirit take not from me. R.
Give me back the joy of your salvation,
    and a willing spirit sustain in me.
O Lord, open my lips,
    and my mouth shall proclaim your praise. R.

Second Reading *(2 Corinthians 5:20–6:2)*

Brothers and sisters: We are **ambassadors** for Christ, as if God were appealing through us. We implore you on behalf of Christ, be **reconciled** to God. For our sake he made him to be sin who did not know sin, so that we might become the righteousness of God in him.

Working together, then, we appeal to you not to receive the grace of God in vain. For he says:

In an acceptable time I heard you,
    and on the day of salvation I helped you.

Behold, now is a very acceptable time; behold, now is the day of salvation.

The word of the Lord. **Thanks be to God.**

Gospel *(Matthew 6:1-6, 16-18)*

A reading from the holy Gospel according to Matthew.
Glory to you, O Lord.

Jesus said to his disciples: "Take care not to perform righteous deeds in order that people may see them; otherwise, you will have no recompense from your heavenly Father. When you give alms, do not blow a trumpet before you, as the hypocrites do in the synagogues and in the streets to win the praise of others. Amen, I say to you, they have received their reward. But when you give **alms**, do not let your left hand know what your right is doing, so that your almsgiving may be secret. And your Father who sees in secret will repay you.

"When you pray, do not be like the **hypocrites**, who love to stand and pray in the synagogues and on street corners so that others may see them. Amen, I say to you, they have received their reward. But when you pray, go to your inner room, close the door, and pray to your Father in secret. And your Father who sees in secret will repay you.

"When you fast, do not look gloomy like the hypocrites. They neglect their appearance, so that they may appear to others to be fasting. Amen, I say to you, they have received their reward. But when you fast, anoint your head and wash your face, so that you may not appear to be fasting, except to your Father who is hidden. And your Father who sees what is hidden will repay you."

The Gospel of the Lord. **Praise to you, Lord Jesus Christ.**

Key Words

Ash Wednesday marks the beginning of Lent. Ashes are used as a sign of our sorrow for having turned away from God; they are placed on our forehead in the sign of the cross and we keep them until they wear off. The ashes are often produced by burning palms from the previous year's Passion (Palm) Sunday celebration.

To **rend** something is to tear it apart forcefully. In biblical times, people would tear their clothing and cover themselves with ashes as signs of their repentance or sorrow. The Prophet Joel is saying that God would rather we rend or open our hearts as a sign of our willingness to return to God.

A **congregation** is a gathering of people, usually for worship. In the Hebrew Scriptures, it can also mean the whole people of God.

Ambassadors are messengers who have special authority to deliver a message or speak on someone else's behalf. Saint Paul is telling us that we have a role to play as followers of Christ: we are chosen to spread the good news. If we are to be faithful messengers, then we must open our hearts and be reconciled to God.

To be **reconciled** means to be "at-one" with someone, by making up for something wrong we may have done. Through his death, Jesus makes up for our sins and we are reconciled with God.

The three traditional Lenten practices are prayer, fasting, and almsgiving. To give **alms** is to give money to the poor. The word comes from the Greek word for compassion or pity. During Lent, we not only focus on our own spiritual life, we also make a special effort to help those around us who are in need.

Hypocrites are people whose actions don't match their words. They may say they love God, but they don't act in a loving way. Such behavior hurts that person, others around them, and God.

MARCH 5
1st Sunday of Lent

First Reading *(Genesis 2:7-9; 3:1-7)*

The LORD God formed man out of the clay of the ground and blew into his nostrils the breath of life, and so man became a living being.

Then the LORD God planted a garden in Eden, in the east, and placed there the man whom he had formed. Out of the ground the Lord God made various trees grow that were delightful to look at and good for food, with the tree of life in the middle of the garden and the tree of the knowledge of **good and evil**.

Now the serpent was the most cunning of all the animals that the LORD God had made. The serpent asked the woman, "Did God really tell you not to eat from any of the trees in the garden?" The woman answered the serpent: "We may eat of the fruit of the trees in the garden; it is only about the fruit of the tree in the middle of the garden that God said, 'You shall not eat it or even touch it, lest you die.' " But the serpent said to the woman: "You certainly will not die! No, God knows well that the moment you eat of it your eyes will be opened and you will be like gods who know what is good and what is evil." The woman saw that the tree was good for food, pleasing to the eyes, and desirable for gaining wisdom. So she took some of its fruit and ate it; and she also gave some to her husband, who was with her, and he ate it. Then the eyes of both of them were opened, and they realized that they were naked; so they sewed fig leaves together and made loincloths for themselves.

The word of the Lord. **Thanks be to God.**

Responsorial Psalm *(Psalm 51:3-4, 5-6, 12-13, 17)*

R. **Be merciful, O Lord, for we have sinned.**

Have mercy on me, O God, in your goodness;
    in the greatness of your compassion
        wipe out my offense.
Thoroughly wash me from my guilt
    and of my sin cleanse me. R.
For I acknowledge my offense,
    and my sin is before me always:
"Against you only have I sinned,
    and done what is evil in your sight." R.
A clean heart create for me, O God,
    and a steadfast spirit renew within me.
Cast me not out from your presence,
    and your Holy Spirit take not from me. R.
Give me back the joy of your salvation,
    and a willing spirit sustain in me.
O LORD, open my lips,
    and my mouth shall proclaim your praise. R.

Second Reading *(Romans 5:12-19)*

For the shorter version, omit the indented parts in brackets.

Brothers and sisters: Through one man sin entered the world, and through sin, death, and thus death came to all men, inasmuch as all sinned.
[—for up to the time of the law, sin was in the world, though sin is not accounted when there is no law. But death reigned from Adam to Moses, even over those who did not sin after the pattern of the trespass of Adam, who is the type of the one who was to come.

But the gift is not like the transgression. For if by the transgression of the one, the many died, how much more did the grace of God and the gracious gift of the one man Jesus Christ overflow for the many. And the gift is not like the result of the one who sinned. For after one sin there was the judgment that brought condemnation; but the gift, after many transgressions, brought acquittal.]

For if, by the transgression of the one, death came to reign through that one, how much more will those who receive the abundance of grace and of the gift of justification come to reign in life through the one Jesus Christ. In conclusion, just as through one transgression condemnation came upon all, so, through one righteous act, acquittal and life came to all. For just as through the disobedience of the one man the many were made sinners, so, through the obedience of the one, the many will be made righteous.

The word of the Lord. **Thanks be to God.**

Gospel *(Matthew 4:1-11)*

A reading from the holy Gospel according to Matthew. **Glory to you, O Lord.**

At that time Jesus was led by the Spirit into the desert to be **tempted** by the devil. He fasted for forty days and forty nights, and afterwards he was hungry. The tempter approached and said to him, "If you are the Son of God, command that these stones become loaves of bread." He said in reply, "It is written:
> One does not live on bread alone,
>> but on every word that comes forth
>> from the mouth of God."

Then the devil took him to the holy city, and made him stand on the **parapet** of the temple, and said to him, "If you are the Son of God, throw yourself down. For it is written:
> He will command his angels concerning you
>> and with their hands they will support you,
> lest you dash your foot against a stone."

Jesus answered him, "Again it is written,
> You shall not put the Lord, your God, to the test."

Then the devil took him up to a very high mountain, and showed him all the kingdoms of the world in their magnificence, and he said to him, "All these I shall give to you, if you will prostrate yourself and **worship** me." At this, Jesus said to him, "Get away, Satan! It is written:
> The Lord, your God, shall you worship
>> and him alone shall you serve."

Then the devil left him and, behold, angels came and ministered to him.

The Gospel of the Lord. **Praise to you, Lord Jesus Christ.**

Key Words

Genesis is the first book of the Bible. It tells many stories, including the stories of creation, Adam and Eve, the Flood, Abraham, and the people's faith in God. These stories help us understand that God loves us and wants us to love him too.

It is hard to understand fully the notions of **good and evil**. In this story from Genesis, we see evil as an enemy of God's, an enemy who tempts us to turn away from our Creator who is all-good.

The letter of Saint Paul to the Romans was written to the small community of Christians who lived in Rome. Saint Paul wanted to visit them, so he sent them this letter ahead of

him, to encourage them and to remind them of the teachings of Jesus.

When we are **tempted**, we think about doing something we know to be wrong. The Spirit of God within us gives us the strength to say no to temptation. Every time we pray the Our Father, we ask God to give us this strength.

The **parapet** of the temple was its highest point. From here, Jesus could see a great distance. It was also dangerously high.

When we **worship** God, we praise him for his love and mercy.

MARCH 12
2nd Sunday of Lent

First Reading *(Genesis 12:1-4a)*

The LORD said to **Abram**: "Go forth from the land of your kinsfolk
and from your father's house to a land that I will show you.
"I will make of you a **great nation**,
    and I will bless you;
I will make your name great,
    so that you will be a blessing.
I will bless those who bless you
    and curse those who curse you.
All the communities of the earth
    shall find blessing in you."

Abram went as the LORD directed him.

The word of the Lord. **Thanks be to God.**

Responsorial Psalm *(Psalm 33:4-5, 18-19, 20, 22)*

R. **Lord, let your mercy be on us,
as we place our trust in you.**

Upright is the word of the LORD,
    and all his works are trustworthy.
He loves justice and right;
    of the kindness of the LORD the earth is full. R.
See, the eyes of the LORD are upon those
        who fear him,
    upon those who hope for his kindness,
to deliver them from death
    and preserve them in spite of famine. R.
Our soul waits for the LORD,
    who is our help and our shield.
May your kindness, O LORD, be upon us
    who have put our hope in you. R.

Second Reading *(2 Timothy 1:8b-10)*

Beloved: Bear your share of hardship for the gospel with the strength that comes from God.

He saved us and **called** us to a holy life, not according to our works but according to his own design and the grace bestowed on us in Christ Jesus before time began, but now made manifest through the appearance of our savior Christ Jesus, who destroyed death and brought life and **immortality** to light through the gospel.

The word of the Lord. **Thanks be to God.**

Gospel *(Matthew 17:1-9)*

A reading from the holy Gospel according to Matthew.
Glory to you, O Lord.

Jesus took Peter, James, and John his brother, and led them up a high mountain by themselves. And he was **transfigured** before them; his face shone like the sun and his clothes became white as light. And behold, Moses and Elijah appeared to them, conversing with him. Then Peter said to Jesus in reply, "Lord, it is good that we are here. If you wish, I will make three tents here, one for you, one for Moses, and one for **Elijah**." While he was still speaking, behold, a bright cloud cast a shadow over them, then from the cloud came a voice that said, "This is my beloved Son, with whom I am well pleased; listen to him." When the disciples heard this, they fell prostrate and were very much afraid. But Jesus came and touched them, saying, "Rise, and do not be afraid." And when the disciples raised their eyes, they saw no one else but Jesus alone.

As they were coming down from the mountain, Jesus charged them, "Do not tell the vision to anyone until the Son of Man has been raised from the dead."

The Gospel of the Lord. **Praise to you, Lord Jesus Christ.**

Abram means "noble father." Abram had true faith in God. God promised that if Abram was faithful to God, he would become the head of a huge family. When he proved his faithfulness, God then gave him a new name: Abraham, which means "father of many."

Abraham's descendants (including us) became a **great nation**, as God had promised. The people of God all over the world are also a great nation, brothers and sisters in Christ.

Timothy was a friend of Saint Paul's. He helped Paul to spread the gospel and was in charge of the Church in Ephesus, Greece. In the New Testament there are two letters to Timothy.

When we live the life Jesus has planned for us, we are responding to his **calling**. Little by little, God opens our ears so that we will hear this call and follow Jesus.

Because Jesus died and rose again, and because we are united with Jesus, we share in his **immortality** (life without death).

When Jesus was **transfigured**, he looked different somehow. His friends saw Jesus as he really is: the Son of God.

The prophet **Elijah** lived about 900 years before Jesus. He is one of the great prophets in the Hebrew Scriptures or Old Testament. He taught the people to believe in God alone.

111

MARCH 19

3rd Sunday of Lent

First Reading *(Exodus 17:3-7)*

In those days, in their thirst for water, the people grumbled against Moses, saying, "Why did you ever make us leave Egypt? Was it just to have us die here of thirst with our children and our livestock?" So Moses cried out to the LORD, "What shall I do with this people? A little more and they will stone me!" The LORD answered Moses, "Go over there in front of the people, along with some of the elders of Israel, holding in your hand, as you go, the **staff** with which you struck the river. I will be standing there in front of you on the rock in Horeb. Strike the rock, and the water will flow from it for the people to drink." This Moses did, in the presence of the elders of Israel. The place was called Massah and Meribah, because the Israelites quarreled there and tested the LORD, saying, "Is the LORD in our midst or not?"

The word of the Lord. **Thanks be to God.**

Responsorial Psalm *(Psalm 95:1-2, 6-7, 8-9)*

R. **If today you hear his voice, harden not your hearts.**

Come, let us sing joyfully to the LORD;
    let us acclaim the Rock of our salvation.
Let us come into his presence with thanksgiving;
    let us joyfully sing psalms to him. R.
Come, let us bow down in worship;
    let us kneel before the LORD who made us.
For he is our God,
    and we are the people he shepherds,
        the flock he guides. R.
Oh, that today you would hear his voice:
    "Harden not your hearts as at Meribah,
    as in the day of Massah in the desert,
where your fathers tempted me;
    they tested me though they had seen my works." R.

113

Second Reading *(Romans 5:1-2, 5-8)*

Brothers and sisters: Since we have been **justified** by faith, we have peace with God through our Lord Jesus Christ, through whom we have gained access by faith to this grace in which we stand, and we boast in **hope** of the glory of God.

And hope does not disappoint, because the love of God has been poured out into our hearts through the Holy Spirit who has been given to us. For Christ, while we were still helpless, died at the appointed time for the ungodly. Indeed, only with difficulty does one die for a just person, though perhaps for a good person one might even find courage to die. But God proves his love for us in that while we were still sinners Christ died for us.

The word of the Lord. **Thanks be to God.**

Gospel *(John 4:5-42)*

For the shorter reading, omit the indented parts in brackets.

A reading from the holy Gospel according to John.
Glory to you, O Lord.

Jesus came to a town of Samaria called Sychar, near the plot of land that **Jacob** had given to his son Joseph. Jacob's well was there. Jesus, tired from his journey, sat down there at the well. It was about noon.

A woman of Samaria came to draw water. Jesus said to her, "Give me a drink." His disciples had gone into the town to buy food. The Samaritan woman said to him, "How can you, a Jew, ask me, a Samaritan woman, for a drink?"—For Jews use nothing in common with Samaritans.—Jesus answered and said to her, "If you knew the gift of God and who is saying to you, 'Give me a drink,' you would have asked him and he would have given you living water." The woman said to him, "Sir, you do not even have a bucket and the cistern is deep; where then can you get this living water? Are you greater than our father Jacob, who gave us this cistern and drank from it himself with his children and his flocks?" Jesus answered and said to her, "Everyone who drinks this water will be thirsty again; but whoever drinks the water I shall give will never thirst; the water I shall give will become in him a spring of water welling up to eternal life." The woman said to him, "Sir, give me this water, so that I may not be thirsty or have to keep coming here to draw water."

[Jesus said to her, "Go call your husband and come back." The woman answered and said to him, "I do not have a husband." Jesus answered her, "You are right in saying, 'I do not have a husband.' For you have had five husbands, and the one you have now is not your husband. What you have said is true." The woman said to him, "Sir,]

I can see that you are a prophet. Our ancestors worshiped on this mountain; but you people say that the place to worship is in Jerusalem." Jesus said to her, "Believe me, woman, the hour is coming when you will worship the Father neither on this mountain nor in Jerusalem. You people worship what you do not understand; we worship what we understand, because salvation is from the Jews. But the hour is coming, and is now here, when true worshipers will **worship the Father in Spirit and truth**; and indeed the Father seeks such people to worship him. God is Spirit, and those who worship him must worship in Spirit and truth." The woman said to him, "I know that the **Messiah** is coming, the one called the Christ; when he comes, he will tell us everything." Jesus said to her, "I am he, the one speaking with you."

[At that moment his disciples returned, and were amazed that he was talking with a woman, but still no one said, "What are you looking for?" or "Why are you talking with her?" The woman left her water jar and went into the town and said to the people, "Come see a man who told me everything I have done. Could he possibly be the Christ?" They went out of the town and came to him. Meanwhile, the disciples urged him, "Rabbi, eat." But he said to them, "I have food to eat of which you do not know." So the disciples said to one another, "Could someone have brought him something to eat?" Jesus said to them, "My food is to do the will of the one who sent me and to finish his work. Do you not say, 'In four months the harvest will be here'? I tell you, look up and see the fields ripe for the harvest. The reaper is already receiving payment and gathering crops for eternal life, so that the sower and reaper can rejoice together. For here the saying is verified that 'One sows and another reaps.' I sent you to reap what you have not worked for; others have done the work, and you are sharing the fruits of their work."]

Many of the Samaritans of that town began to believe in him [because of the word of the woman who testified, "He told me everything I have done."] When the Samaritans came to him, they invited him to stay with them; and he stayed there two days.

Many more began to believe in him because of his word, and they said to the woman, "We no longer believe because of your word; for we have heard for ourselves, and we know that this is truly the savior of the world."

The Gospel of the Lord. **Praise to you, Lord Jesus Christ.**

Key Words

The book of **Exodus** is the second book of the Bible. It tells the story of how God freed his people from slavery in Egypt. God made a promise or covenant with his people and gave them the Ten Commandments to show them how to live well.

A **staff** is large stick or cane used by a shepherd and other herdsmen. It can also be used as a walking stick. It is a symbol of authority carried by a leader. A bishop carries a staff called a crozier.

When we hurt others, we break our friendship with God. Jesus came to restore our friendship with God, and we are **justified** or brought back to God by our faith in Jesus.

We have **hope** or confidence that God will fulfill his promises. Hope is one of the three great Christian virtues. The other two are faith and love.

The holy Gospel according to John tells us about the life, death, and resurrection of Jesus. It was written about 60 years after Jesus died. Saint John's gospel includes some stories and sayings that are not in the other three gospels (Matthew, Mark, and Luke).

Jacob, also called Israel, was the son of Isaac and the grandson of Abraham. The twelve tribes of Israel are all descended from Jacob.

When Jesus says to **worship the Father in spirit and truth**, he is reminding us that God does not want us to bring a sacrifice or gift when we worship. God would rather we bring our hearts full of love.

Jesus and his disciples spoke Aramaic. **Messiah** is an Aramaic word meaning "anointed." The chosen person was anointed or blessed with holy oil and given a special mission. The Greek word for "anointed" is "Christ."

MARCH 26
4th Sunday of Lent

First Reading *(1 Samuel 16:1b, 6-7, 10-13a)*

The LORD said to Samuel: "Fill your horn with oil, and be on your way. I am sending you to Jesse of Bethlehem, for I have chosen my king from among his sons."

As Jesse and his sons came to the sacrifice, Samuel looked at Eliab and thought, "Surely the LORD's anointed is here before him." But the LORD said to Samuel: "Do not judge from his appearance or from his lofty stature, because I have rejected him. Not as man sees does God see, because man sees the appearance but the LORD looks into the heart." In the same way Jesse presented seven sons before Samuel, but Samuel said to Jesse, "The LORD has not chosen any one of these." Then Samuel asked Jesse, "Are these all the sons you have?" Jesse replied, "There is still the youngest, who is tending the sheep." Samuel said to Jesse, "Send for him; we will not begin the sacrificial banquet until he arrives here." Jesse sent and had the young man brought to them. He was ruddy, a youth handsome to behold and making a splendid appearance. The LORD said, "There—**anoint** him, for this is the one!" Then Samuel, with the horn of oil in hand, anointed David in the presence of his brothers; and from that day on, the spirit of the LORD rushed upon David.

The word of the Lord. **Thanks be to God.**

Responsorial Psalm *(Psalm 23:1-3a, 3b-4, 5, 6)*

R. **The Lord is my shepherd; there is nothing I shall want.**

The LORD IS my shepherd; I shall not want.
   In verdant pastures he gives me repose;
beside restful waters he leads me;
   he refreshes my soul. R.
He guides me in right paths
   for his name's sake.
Even though I walk in the dark valley
   I fear no evil; for you are at my side
with your rod and your staff
   that give me courage. R.

You spread the table before me
    in the sight of my foes;
you anoint my head with oil;
    my cup overflows. R̶.
Only goodness and kindness follow me
    all the days of my life;
and I shall dwell in the house of the Lᴏʀᴅ
    for years to come. R̶.

Second Reading *(Ephesians 5:8-14)*

Brothers and sisters: You were once darkness, but now you are light in the Lord. Live as children of light, for light produces every kind of goodness and righteousness and truth. Try to learn what is pleasing to the Lord. Take no part in the fruitless works of darkness; rather expose them, for it is shameful even to mention the things done by them in secret; but everything exposed by the light becomes visible, for everything that becomes visible is light. Therefore, it says:
    "Awake, O sleeper,
    and arise from the dead,
    and Christ will give you light."

The word of the Lord. **Thanks be to God.**

Gospel *(John 9:1-41)*

For the shorter version, omit the indented parts in brackets.

A reading from the holy Gospel according to John.
Glory to you, O Lord.

As Jesus passed by he saw a man **blind** from birth.
    [His disciples asked him, "Rabbi, who sinned, this man
    or his parents, that he was born blind?" Jesus answered,
    "Neither he nor his parents sinned; it is so that the works
    of God might be made visible through him. We have to do
    the works of the one who sent me while it is day. Night is
    coming when no one can work. While I am in the world, I
    am the light of the world." When he had said this,]
he spat on the ground and made clay with the saliva, and smeared the clay on his eyes, and said to him, "Go wash in the

Pool of Siloam"—which means Sent—. So he went and washed, and came back able to see.

His neighbors and those who had seen him earlier as a beggar said, "Isn't this the one who used to sit and beg?" Some said, "It is," but others said, "No, he just looks like him." He said, "I am."

[So they said to him, "How were your eyes opened?" He replied, "The man called Jesus made clay and anointed my eyes and told me, 'Go to Siloam and wash.' So I went there and washed and was able to see." And they said to him, "Where is he?" He said, "I don't know."]

They brought the one who was once blind to the **Pharisees**. Now Jesus had made clay and opened his eyes on a sabbath. So then the Pharisees also asked him how he was able to see. He said to them, "He put clay on my eyes, and I washed, and now I can see." So some of the Pharisees said, "This man is not from God, because he does not keep the **sabbath**." But others said, "How can a sinful man do such signs?" And there was a division among them. So they said to the blind man again, "What do you have to say about him, since he opened your eyes?" He said, "He is a prophet."

[Now the Jews did not believe that he had been blind and gained his sight until they summoned the parents of the one who had gained his sight. They asked them, "Is this your son, who you say was born blind? How does he now see?" His parents answered and said, "We know that this is our son and that he was born blind. We do not know how he sees now, nor do we know who opened his eyes. Ask him, he is of age; he can speak for himself." His parents said this because they were afraid of the Jews, for the Jews had already agreed that if anyone acknowledged him as the Christ, he would be expelled from the synagogue. For this reason his parents said, "He is of age; question him."

So a second time they called the man who had been blind and said to him, "Give God the praise! We know that this man is a sinner." He replied, "If he is a sinner, I do not know. One thing I do know is that I was blind and now I see." So they said to him, "What did he do to you? How did he open your eyes?" He answered them, "I told you already and you did not listen. Why do you want to hear it again? Do you want to become his disciples, too?" They ridiculed him and said, "You are that man's disciple; we are disciples of Moses! We know that God spoke to Moses, but we do not know where this one is from." The man answered and said to them, "This is what is so amazing, that you do not know where he is from, yet he opened my eyes. We know that God does not listen to sinners, but if one is devout and does his will, he listens to him. It is unheard of that anyone ever opened the eyes of a person born blind. If this man were not from God, he would not be able to do anything."]

They answered and said to him, "You were born totally in sin, and are you trying to teach us?" Then they threw him out.

When Jesus heard that they had thrown him out, he found him and said, "Do you believe in the Son of Man?" He answered and said, "Who is he, sir, that I may believe in him?" Jesus said to him, "You have seen him, the one speaking with you is he." He said, "I do believe, Lord," and he worshiped him.

[Then Jesus said, "I came into this world for judgment, so that those who do not see might see, and those who do see might become blind."

Some of the Pharisees who were with him heard this and said to him, "Surely we are not also blind, are we?" Jesus said to them, "If you were blind, you would have no sin; but now you are saying, 'We see,' so your sin remains."]

The Gospel of the Lord. **Praise to you, Lord Jesus Christ.**

Key Words

Samuel, a prophet and judge in Israel, was born over 1,000 years before Jesus. The Lord chose Samuel to **anoint** Saul, the first king of Israel. Samuel also anointed David, who was king after Saul. The Bible contains two books in his name: 1 Samuel and 2 Samuel.

To **anoint** means to bless with oil. In the Bible it can also mean to give someone a mission, an important job. Christians are anointed at baptism and confirmation, we anoint people when they are very sick, and priests and bishops are anointed at their ordination: our mission is to love people as God loves them.

The **Ephesians** were a group of Christians in the city of Ephesus. A letter Saint Paul wrote to them is now part of the Bible. Ephesus is located in modern-day Turkey.

In the time of Jesus, if someone was born **blind**, people assumed this was because God was punishing the parents for something they had done wrong. Jesus says this is not true and then heals the man born blind to show that Jesus has power over evil.

The **Pharisees** were Jewish leaders who tried to follow the letter of the law, but sometimes forgot to live by love. Jesus pointed out this lack of love.

The **Sabbath** is the day of the week when human beings rest as God did on the seventh day of creation. It is a chance for us to spend time praising God and enjoying creation. One of the Ten Commandments instructs us to keep the Sabbath holy.

First Reading *(Ezekiel 37:12-14)*

Thus says the Lord God: O my people, I will **open your graves** and have you rise from them, and bring you back to the land of Israel. Then you shall know that I am the LORD, when I open your graves and have you rise from them, O my people! I will put my spirit in you that you may live, and I will settle you upon your land; thus you shall know that I am the **LORD**. I have promised, and I will do it, says the LORD.

The word of the Lord. **Thanks be to God.**

Responsorial Psalm *(Psalm 130:1-2, 3-4, 5-6, 7-8)*

R. **With the Lord there is mercy and fullness of redemption.**

Out of the depths I cry to you, O LORD;
    LORD, hear my voice!
Let your ears be attentive
    to my voice in supplication. R.
If you, O LORD, mark iniquities,
    LORD, who can stand?
But with you is forgiveness,
    that you may be revered. R.
I trust in the LORD;
    my soul trusts in his word.
More than sentinels wait for the dawn,
    let Israel wait for the LORD. R.
For with the LORD is kindness
    and with him is plenteous redemption;
and he will **redeem** Israel
    from all their iniquities. R.

Second Reading *(Romans 8:8-11)*

Brothers and sisters: Those who are in the flesh cannot please God. But you are not in the flesh; on the contrary, you are in the spirit, if only the Spirit of God dwells in you. Whoever does not have the Spirit of Christ does not belong to him. But if Christ is in you, although the body is dead because of sin, the spirit is alive because of righteousness. If the **Spirit of the One** who raised

Jesus from the dead dwells in you, the One who raised Christ from the dead will give life to your mortal bodies also, through his Spirit dwelling in you.

The word of the Lord. **Thanks be to God.**

Gospel *(John 11:1-45)*

For the shorter version, omit the indented parts in brackets and add the text in parentheses.

A reading from the holy Gospel according to John.
Glory to you, O Lord.

> [Now a man was ill, Lazarus from Bethany, the village of Mary and her sister Martha. Mary was the one who had anointed the Lord with perfumed oil and dried his feet with her hair; it was her brother Lazarus who was ill. So]

The **sisters (of Lazarus)** sent word to Jesus saying, "Master, the one you love is ill." When Jesus heard this he said, "This illness is not to end in death, but is for the glory of God, that the Son of God may be glorified through it." Now Jesus loved Martha and her sister and Lazarus. So when he heard that he was ill, he remained for two days in the place where he was. Then after this he said to his disciples, "Let us go back to Judea."

> [The disciples said to him, "Rabbi, the Jews were just trying to stone you, and you want to go back there?" Jesus answered, "Are there not twelve hours in a day? If one walks during the day, he does not stumble, because he sees the light of this world. But if one walks at night, he stumbles, because the light is not in him." He said this, and then told them, "Our friend Lazarus is asleep, but I am going to awaken him." So the disciples said to him, "Master, if he is asleep, he will be saved." But Jesus was talking about his death, while they thought that he meant ordinary sleep. So then Jesus said to them clearly, "Lazarus has died. And I am glad for you that I was not there, that you may believe. Let us go to him." So Thomas, called Didymus, said to his fellow disciples, "Let us also go to die with him."]

When Jesus arrived, he found that Lazarus had already been in the tomb for four days.

[Now Bethany was near Jerusalem, only about two miles away. And many of the Jews had come to Martha and Mary to comfort them about their brother.]

When Martha heard that Jesus was coming, she went to meet him; but Mary sat at home. Martha said to Jesus, "Lord, if you had been here, my brother would not have died. But even now I know that whatever you ask of God, God will give you." Jesus said to her, "Your brother **will rise**." Martha said to him, "I know he will rise, in the resurrection on the last day." Jesus told her, "I am the resurrection and the life; whoever believes in me, even if he dies, will live, and everyone who lives and believes in me will never die. Do you believe this?" She said to him, "Yes, Lord. I have come to believe that you are the Christ, the Son of God, the one who is coming into the world."

[When she had said this, she went and called her sister Mary secretly, saying, "The teacher is here and is asking for you." As soon as she heard this, she rose quickly and went to him. For Jesus had not yet come into the village, but was still where Martha had met him. So when the Jews who were with her in the house comforting her saw Mary get up quickly and go out, they followed her, presuming that she was going to the tomb to weep there. When Mary came to where Jesus was and saw him, she fell at his feet and said to him, "Lord, if you had been here, my brother would not have died." When Jesus saw her weeping and the Jews who had come with her weeping,]

He became perturbed and deeply troubled, and said, "Where have you laid him?" They said to him, "Sir, come and see." And Jesus wept. So the Jews said, "See how he loved him." But some of them said, "Could not the one who opened the eyes of the blind man have done something so that this man would not have died?"

So Jesus, perturbed again, came to the tomb. It was a cave, and a stone lay across it. Jesus said, "Take away the stone." Martha, the dead man's sister, said to him, "Lord, by now there will be a stench; he has been dead for four days." Jesus said to her, "Did I not tell you that if you believe you will see the glory of God?" So they took away the stone. And Jesus raised his eyes and said, "Father, I thank you for hearing me. I know that you always hear me; but because of the crowd here I have said this, that they may believe that you sent me." And when he had said this, He cried out in a loud voice, "Lazarus, come out!" The dead man came out, tied hand and foot with burial bands, and his face was wrapped in a cloth. So Jesus said to them, "Untie him and let him go."

Now many of the Jews who had come to Mary and seen what he had done began to believe in him.

The Gospel of the Lord. **Praise to you, Lord Jesus Christ.**

Key Words

Ezekiel was one of the most important prophets in Israel. He lived during a time when many of the people of Jerusalem were taken prisoner and forced to live in exile in Babylon. The king and Ezekiel were taken away, too. Ezekiel helped the people follow God's ways even though they were far from home.

The people of Israel lived in exile in Babylon and were very unhappy. Through the prophet Ezekiel, God promised to bring the people back to Israel. God said, "I am going to **open your graves**" and bring new life to the dry, dead bones of the people of Israel.

To **redeem** is to buy something back or to pay to free someone. God is called our Redeemer because God freed Israel from slavery in Egypt. Christ is our Redeemer, for by his resurrection he freed us from the power of death.

In the Bible, God is called the **Lord** because God is more powerful than all human power.

The **Spirit of the One**, or the Holy Spirit, is the third person of the Holy Trinity. The Spirit of God is always present in our hearts and in the Church, helping us to live like brothers and sisters.

The **sisters of Lazarus** were Martha and Mary, and all three were Jesus' friends. They lived in Bethany, just a few miles from Jerusalem. When Jesus had visited them before, he had reminded the sisters that it was more important to listen to the word of God than to worry about daily chores.

When Jesus says that Lazarus **will rise** again, he is speaking of the resurrection of the dead when Jesus comes again at the end of time.

APRIL 9
**Palm Sunday of the
Passion of the Lord**

Gospel *(Matthew 21:1-11)*

A reading from the holy Gospel according to Matthew.
Glory to you, O Lord.

When Jesus and the disciples drew near Jerusalem and
came to Bethphage on the Mount of Olives, Jesus sent two
disciples, saying to them, "Go into the village opposite you, and
immediately you will find an ass tethered, and a colt with her.
Untie them and bring them here to me. And if anyone should say
anything to you, reply, 'The master has need of them.' Then he
will send them at once." This happened so that what had been
spoken through the prophet might be fulfilled:

> "*Say to* **daughter Zion,**
> '*Behold, your king comes to you,*
>   *meek and riding on an ass,*
>   *and on a colt, the foal of a beast of burden.*' "

The disciples went and did as Jesus had ordered them. They
brought the ass and the colt and laid their cloaks over them, and
he sat upon them. The very large crowd spread their cloaks on
the road, while others cut branches from the trees and strewed
them on the road. The crowds preceding him and those following
kept crying out and saying:

> "**Hosanna** to the **Son of David**;
>   blessed is the he who comes in the name of the Lord;
> hosanna in the highest."

And when he entered Jerusalem the whole city was shaken and
asked, "Who is this?" And the crowds replied, "This is Jesus the
prophet, from Nazareth in Galilee."

The Gospel of the Lord. **Praise to you, Lord Jesus Christ.**

First Reading *(Isaiah 50:4-7)*

> The Lord GOD has given me
>   a well-trained tongue,
> that I might know how to **speak to the weary**
>   a word that will rouse them.
> Morning after morning
>   he opens my ear that I may hear;
> and I have not rebelled,
>   have not turned back.
> I gave my back to those who beat me,
>   my cheeks to those who plucked my beard;

my face I did not shield
from buffets and spitting.

The Lord GOD is my help,
therefore I am not disgraced;
I have set my face like flint,
knowing that I shall not be put to shame.

The word of the Lord. **Thanks be to God.**

Responsorial Psalm *(Psalm 22:8-9, 17-18, 19-20, 23-24)*

R. **My God, my God, why have you abandoned me?**

All who see me scoff at me;
they mock me with parted lips, they wag their heads:
"He relied on the LORD; let him deliver him,
let him rescue him, if he loves him." R.
Indeed, many dogs surround me,
a pack of evildoers closes in upon me;
they have pierced my hands and my feet;
I can count all my bones. R.
They divide my garments among them,
and for my vesture they cast lots.
But you, O LORD, be not far from me;
O my help, hasten to aid me. R.
I will proclaim your name to my brethren;
in the midst of the assembly I will praise you:
"You who fear the LORD, praise him;
all you descendants of Jacob, give glory to him;
revere him, all you descendants of Israel!" R.

Second Reading *(Philippians 2:6-11)*

Christ Jesus, though he was in the form of God,
did not regard equality with God
something to be grasped.
Rather, he emptied himself,
taking the form of a slave,
coming in human likeness;
and found human in appearance,
he humbled himself,

becoming obedient to the point of death,
   even death on a cross.
Because of this, God greatly exalted him
   and bestowed on him the name
   which is above every name,
   that at the name of Jesus
   every knee should bend,
   of those in heaven and on earth and under the earth,
   and every tongue confess that
   Jesus Christ is Lord,
   to the glory of God the Father.

The word of the Lord. **Thanks be to God.**

Gospel *(Matthew 26:14–27:66)*

*Several readers may proclaim the passion narrative today. (N)
indicates the narrator, (†) the words of Jesus, (V) a voice, and (C)
the crowd. The shorter version begins (page 136) and ends (page 139)
at the asterisks.*

N The **Passion** of our Lord Jesus Christ according to Matthew.
   One of the Twelve, who was called Judas Iscariot, went to
   the chief priests and said,

V "What are you willing to give me if I hand him over to you?"

N They paid him thirty pieces of silver, and from that time on
   he looked for an opportunity to hand him over.
   On the first day of the Feast of Unleavened Bread, the
   disciples approached Jesus and said,

V "Where do you want us to prepare for you to eat the
   Passover"?

N He said,

† "Go into the city to a certain man and tell him,
   'The teacher says, "My appointed time draws near; in your
   house I shall celebrate the Passover with my disciples." ' "

N The disciples then did as Jesus had ordered, and prepared the
   Passover.
   When it was evening, he reclined at table with the Twelve.
   And while they were eating, he said,

† "Amen, I say to you, one of you will betray me."

N Deeply distressed at this, they began to say to him one after another,

V "Surely it is not I, Lord?"

N He said in reply,

† "He who has dipped his hand into the dish with me is the one who will betray me. The Son of Man indeed goes, as it is written of him, but woe to that man by whom the Son of Man is betrayed. It would be better for that man if he had never been born."

N Then Judas, his betrayer, said in reply,

V "Surely it is not I, Rabbi?"

N He answered,

† "You have said so."

N While they were eating, Jesus took bread, said the blessing, broke it, and giving it to his disciples said,

† "Take and eat; this is my body."

N Then he took a cup, gave thanks, and gave it to them, saying,

† "Drink from it, all of you, for this is my blood of the covenant, which will be shed on behalf of many for the forgiveness of sins. I tell you, from now on I shall not drink this fruit of the vine until the day when I drink it with you new in the kingdom of my Father."

N Then, after singing a hymn, they went out to the Mount of Olives.

N Then Jesus said to them,

† "This night all of you will have your faith in me shaken, for it is written:
I will strike the shepherd,
  and the sheep of the flock will be dispersed;
but after I have been raised up, I shall go before you to Galilee."

N Peter said to him in reply,

V "Though all may have their faith in you shaken, mine will never be."

N Jesus said to him,

† "Amen, I say to you, this very night before the cock crows, you will deny me three times."

N Peter said to him,

V "Even though I should have to die with you, I will not deny you."

N And all the disciples spoke likewise.
    Then Jesus came with them to a place called Gethsemane, and he said to his disciples,

† "Sit here while I go over there and pray."

N He took along Peter and the two sons of Zebedee, and began to feel sorrow and distress. Then he said to them,

† "My soul is sorrowful even to death. Remain here and keep watch with me."

N He advanced a little and fell prostrate in prayer, saying,

† "My Father, if it is possible, let this cup pass from me; yet, not as I will, but as you will."

N When he returned to his disciples he found them asleep. He said to Peter,

† "So you could not keep watch with me for one hour? Watch and pray that you may not undergo the test. The spirit is willing, but the flesh is weak."

N Withdrawing a second time, he prayed again,

† "My Father, if it is not possible that this cup pass without my drinking it, your will be done!"

N Then he returned once more and found them asleep, for they could not keep their eyes open. He left them and withdrew again and prayed a third time, saying the same thing again. Then he returned to his disciples and said to them,

† "Are you still sleeping and taking your rest? Behold, the hour is at hand when the Son of Man is to be handed over to sinners. Get up, let us go. Look, my betrayer is at hand."

N While he was still speaking, Judas, one of the Twelve, arrived, accompanied by a large crowd, with swords and clubs, who had come from the chief priests and the elders of the people. His betrayer had arranged a sign with them, saying,

V "The man I shall kiss is the one; arrest him."

N Immediately he went over to Jesus and said,

V "Hail, Rabbi!"

N and he kissed him. Jesus answered him,

† "Friend, do what you have come for."

N Then stepping forward they laid hands on Jesus and arrested him. And behold, one of those who accompanied Jesus put his hand to his sword, drew it, and struck the high priest' s servant, cutting off his ear. Then Jesus said to him,

† "Put your sword back into its sheath, for all who take the sword will perish by the sword. Do you think that I cannot call upon my Father and he will not provide me at this moment with more than twelve legions of angels? But then how would the Scriptures be fulfilled which say that it must come to pass in this way?"

N At that hour Jesus said to the crowds,

† "Have you come out as against a robber, with swords and clubs to seize me? Day after day I sat teaching in the temple area, yet you did not arrest me. But all this has come to pass that the writings of the prophets may be fulfilled."

N Then all the disciples left him and fled.
Those who had arrested Jesus led him away to Caiaphas the high priest, where the scribes and the elders were assembled. Peter was following him at a distance as far as the high priest's courtyard, and going inside he sat down with the servants to see the outcome. The chief priests and the entire Sanhedrin kept trying to obtain false testimony against Jesus in order to put him to death, but they found none, though many false witnesses came forward. Finally two came forward who stated,

C **"This man said, 'I can destroy the temple of God and within three days rebuild it.' "**

N The high priest rose and addressed him,

V   "Have you no answer? What are these men testifying against you?"

N   But Jesus was silent. Then the high priest said to him,

V   "I order you to tell us under oath before the living God whether you are the Christ, the Son of God."

N   Jesus said to him in reply,

†   "You have said so. But I tell you:
       From now on you will see 'the Son of Man
          seated at the right hand of the Power'
          and 'coming on the clouds of heaven.' "

N   Then the high priest tore his robes and said,

V   "He has blasphemed! What further need have we of witnesses? You have now heard the blasphemy; what is your opinion?"

N   They said in reply,

C   **"He deserves to die!"**

N   Then they spat in his face and struck him, while some slapped him, saying,

C   **"Prophesy for us, Christ: who is it that struck you?"**

N   Now Peter was sitting outside in the courtyard. One of the maids came over to him and said,

C   **"You too were with Jesus the Galilean."**

N   But he denied it in front of everyone, saying,

V   "I do not know what you are talking about!"

N   As he went out to the gate, another girl saw him and said to those who were there,

C   **"This man was with Jesus the Nazorean."**

N   Again he denied it with an oath,

V   "I do not know the man!"

N   A little later the bystanders came over and said to Peter,

C   **"Surely you too are one of them; even your speech gives you away."**

N At that he began to curse and to swear,

V "I do not know the man."

N And immediately a cock crowed. Then Peter remembered the word that Jesus had spoken: "Before the cock crows you will deny me three times." He went out and began to weep bitterly.

N When it was morning, all the chief priests and the elders of the people took counsel against Jesus to put him to death. They bound him, led him away, and handed him over to Pilate, the governor.

Then Judas, his betrayer, seeing that Jesus had been condemned, deeply regretted what he had done. He returned the thirty pieces of silver to the chief priests and elders, saying,

V "I have sinned in betraying innocent blood."

N They said,

C **"What is that to us? Look to it yourself."**

N Flinging the money into the temple, he departed and went off and hanged himself. The chief priests gathered up the money, but said,

C **"It is not lawful to deposit this in the temple treasury, for it is the price of blood."**

N After consultation, they used it to buy the potter's field as a burial place for foreigners. That is why that field even today is called the Field of Blood. Then was fulfilled what had been said through Jeremiah the prophet, *And they took the thirty pieces of silver, the value of a man with a price on his head, a price set by some of the Israelites, and they paid it out for the potter's field just as the Lord had commanded me.*

* * *

N [Now] Jesus stood before the governor (Pontius Pilate), and he questioned him,

V "Are you the king of the Jews?"

N Jesus said,

† "You say so."

N And when he was accused by the chief priests and elders, he made no answer. Then Pilate said to him,

V "Do you not hear how many things they are testifying against you?"

N But he did not answer him one word, so that the governor was greatly amazed.

   Now on the occasion of the feast the governor was accustomed to release to the crowd one prisoner whom they wished. And at that time they had a notorious prisoner called Barabbas. So when they had assembled, Pilate said to them,

V "Which one do you want me to release to you, Barabbas, or Jesus called Christ?"

N For he knew that it was out of envy that they had handed him over. While he was still seated on the bench, his wife sent him a message, "Have nothing to do with that righteous man. I suffered much in a dream today because of him." The chief priests and the elders persuaded the crowds to ask for Barabbas but to destroy Jesus. The governor said to them in reply,

V "Which of the two do you want me to release to you?"

N They answered,

C **"Barabbas!"**

N Pilate said to them,

V "Then what shall I do with Jesus called Christ?"

N They all said,

C **"Let him be crucified!"**

N But he said,

V "Why? What evil has he done?"

N They only shouted the louder,

C **"Let him be crucified!"**

N When Pilate saw that he was not succeeding at all, but that a riot was breaking out instead, he took water and washed his hands in the sight of the crowd, saying,

V "I am innocent of this man's blood. Look to it yourselves."

N And the whole people said in reply,

C **"His blood be upon us and upon our children."**

N Then he released Barabbas to them, but after he had Jesus scourged, he handed him over to be crucified.

Then the soldiers of the governor took Jesus inside the praetorium and gathered the whole cohort around him. They stripped off his clothes and threw a scarlet military cloak about him. Weaving a crown out of thorns, they placed it on his head, and a reed in his right hand. And kneeling before him, they mocked him, saying,

C **"Hail, King of the Jews!"**

N They spat upon him and took the reed and kept striking him on the head. And when they had mocked him, they stripped him of the cloak, dressed him in his own clothes, and led him off to crucify him.

As they were going out, they met a Cyrenian named Simon; this man they pressed into service to carry his cross.

And when they came to a place called Golgotha—which means Place of the Skull—, they gave Jesus wine to drink mixed with gall. But when he had tasted it, he refused to drink. After they had crucified him, they divided his garments by casting lots; then they sat down and kept watch over him there. And they placed over his head the written charge against him: This is Jesus, the King of the Jews. Two revolutionaries were crucified with him, one on his right and the other on his left. Those passing by reviled him, shaking their heads and saying,

C **"You who would destroy the temple and rebuild it in three days, save yourself, if you are the Son of God, and come down from the cross!"**

N Likewise the chief priests with the scribes and elders mocked him and said,

C **"He saved others; he cannot save himself. So he is the king of Israel! Let him come down from the cross now, and we will believe in him. He trusted in God; let him deliver him now if he wants him. For he said, 'I am the Son of God.' "**

N The revolutionaries who were crucified with him also kept abusing him in the same way.

From noon onward, darkness came over the whole land until three in the afternoon. And about three o'clock Jesus cried out in a loud voice,

† *"Eli, Eli, lema sabachthani?"*

N which means,

† "My God, my God, why have you forsaken me?"

N Some of the bystanders who heard it said,

C **"This one is calling for Elijah."**

N Immediately one of them ran to get a sponge; he soaked it in wine, and putting it on a reed, gave it to him to drink. But the rest said,

C **"Wait, let us see if Elijah comes to save him."**

N But Jesus cried out again in a loud voice, and gave up his spirit.

Here all kneel and pause for a short time.

N And behold, the veil of the sanctuary was torn in two from top to bottom. The earth quaked, rocks were split, tombs were opened, and the bodies of many saints who had fallen asleep were raised. And coming forth from their tombs after his resurrection, they entered the holy city and appeared to many. The centurion and the men with him who were keeping watch over Jesus feared greatly when they saw the earthquake and all that was happening, and they said,

C **"Truly, this was the Son of God!"**

* * *

N There were many women there, looking on from a distance, who had followed Jesus from Galilee, ministering to him. Among them were Mary Magdalene and Mary the mother of James and Joseph, and the mother of the sons of Zebedee.

When it was evening, there came a rich man from Arimathea named Joseph, who was himself a disciple of Jesus. He went to Pilate and asked for the body of Jesus; then

Pilate ordered it to be handed over. Taking the body, Joseph wrapped it in clean linen and laid it in his new tomb that he had hewn in the rock. Then he rolled a huge stone across the entrance to the tomb and departed. But Mary Magdalene and the other Mary remained sitting there, facing the tomb.

The next day, the one following the day of preparation, the chief priests and the Pharisees gathered before Pilate and said,

C **"Sir, we remember that this impostor while still alive said, 'After three days I will be raised up.' Give orders, then, that the grave be secured until the third day, lest his disciples come and steal him and say to the people, 'He has been raised from the dead.' This last imposture would be worse than the first."**

N Pilate said to them,

V "The guard is yours; go, secure it as best you can."

N So they went and secured the tomb by fixing a seal to the stone and setting the guard.

The Gospel of the Lord. **Praise to you, Lord Jesus Christ.**

Holy Week begins on **Passion Sunday**, which is also called Palm Sunday. On this day we recall Jesus' arrival in Jerusalem, where people greeted him in the streets like a hero, shouting and waving palm branches. During the gospel, we listen to the whole story of Jesus' last days on earth.

Zion was the name of a hill in Jerusalem where the temple was built, but the city itself was often called Zion. **Daughter Zion** is another way of naming the entire nation, the whole People of God.

Hosanna is a Hebrew word that means "save us." When the people in Jerusalem shout it as Jesus approaches, they are saying that they know he is the Messiah who has come to save them.

Son of David (or descendant of King David) is a name people used to describe the Messiah who was to come. It is one of the many names given to Jesus in the Bible.

An important task of a prophet (and also of the Church and all Christians) is to **speak to the weary**—to give strength to those who have fallen or who are weak, to offer hope to the hopeless and comfort to the lonely, and to bring consolation to those who mourn.

The **Passion** of Jesus is the story of the last hours of his earthly life. It begins with the Last Supper and ends when his body is placed in the tomb. When we speak of the "passion" of Jesus, we mean his suffering.

First Reading *(Acts 10:34a, 37-43)*

Peter proceeded to speak and said: "You know what has happened all over Judea, beginning in Galilee after the baptism that John preached, how God **anointed** Jesus of Nazareth with the Holy Spirit and power. He went about doing good and healing all those oppressed by the devil, for God was with him. We are witnesses of all that he did both in the country of the Jews and in Jerusalem. They put him to death by hanging him on a tree. **This man God raised** on the third day and granted that he be visible, not to all the people, but to us, the witnesses chosen by God in advance, who ate and drank with him after he rose from the dead. He commissioned us to preach to the people and testify that he is the one appointed by God as judge of the living and the dead. To him all the **prophets** bear witness, that everyone who believes in him will receive forgiveness of sins through his name."

The word of the Lord. **Thanks be to God.**

Responsorial Psalm *(Psalm 118:1-2, 16-17, 22-23)*

R̶. **This is the day the Lord has made; let us rejoice and be glad.** *Or* **Alleluia!**

Give thanks to the LORD, for he is good,
for his mercy endures forever.
Let the house of Israel say,
"His mercy endures forever." R̶.
"The right hand of the LORD has struck with power;
the right hand of the LORD is exalted.
I shall not die, but live,
and declare the works of the LORD." R̶.
The stone which the builders rejected
has become the cornerstone.
By the LORD has this been done;
it is wonderful in our eyes. R̶.

An alternate reading follows.

Second Reading *(Colossians 3:1-4)*

Brothers and sisters: If then you were raised with Christ, seek **what is above**, where Christ is seated at the right hand of God. Think of what is above, not of what is on earth. For you have died, and your life is hidden with Christ in God. When Christ your life appears, then you too will appear with him in glory.

The word of the Lord. **Thanks be to God.**

OR

Second Reading *(1 Corinthians 5:6b-8)*

Brothers and sisters: Do you not know that a little yeast leavens all the dough? Clear out the old yeast, so that you may become a fresh batch of dough, inasmuch as you are unleavened. For our paschal lamb, Christ, has been sacrificed. Therefore, let us celebrate the feast, not with the old yeast, the yeast of malice and wickedness, but with the unleavened bread of sincerity and truth.

The word of the Lord. **Thanks be to God.**

Sequence

Christians, to the Paschal Victim
    Offer your thankful praises!
A Lamb the sheep redeems;
    Christ, who only is sinless,
    Reconciles sinners to the Father.
Death and life have contended in that combat stupendous:
    The Prince of life, who died, reigns immortal.
Speak, Mary, declaring
    What you saw, wayfaring.
"The tomb of Christ, who is living,
    The glory of Jesus' resurrection;
Bright angels attesting,
    The shroud and napkin resting.
Yes, Christ my hope is arisen;
    To Galilee he goes before you."

Christ indeed from death is risen, our new life obtaining.
   Have mercy, victor King, ever reigning!
      Amen. Alleluia.

For an alternate gospel reading for an afternoon or evening Mass, use Luke 24:13-35. Matthew 28:1-10 may also be used.

Gospel *(John 20:1-9)*

A reading from the holy Gospel according to John.
Glory to you, O Lord.

On the first day of the week, Mary of Magdala came to the tomb early in the morning, while it was still dark, and saw the stone removed from the tomb. So she ran and went to Simon Peter and to the other disciple whom Jesus loved, and told them, "They have taken the Lord from the tomb, and we don't know where they put him." So Peter and the other disciple went out and came to the tomb. They both ran, but the other disciple ran faster than Peter and arrived at the tomb first; he bent down and saw the burial cloths there, but did not go in. When Simon Peter arrived after him, he went into the tomb and saw the **burial cloths** there, and the cloth that had covered his head, not with the burial cloths but rolled up in a separate place. Then the other disciple also went in, the one who had arrived at the tomb first, and he saw and believed. For they did not yet understand the Scripture that he had to rise from the dead.

The Gospel of the Lord. **Praise to you, Lord Jesus Christ.**

The **Acts of the Apostles** is a book in the New Testament that describes how the Church grew after Jesus rose from the dead. It was written by Saint Luke, who also wrote a gospel.

To **anoint** means to bless with oil. In the Bible it can also mean to give someone a mission, an important job. God anoints Jesus with the Holy Spirit to show that God was giving Jesus his mission. Christians are anointed at baptism and confirmation, we anoint people when they are very sick, and priests and bishops are anointed at their ordination: our mission is to live as Jesus taught us.

This man God raised: Jesus' resurrection, his passing through death to eternal life, is the most important element of the Christian faith. We believe that Jesus did not remain dead in the tomb, but overcame death, suffering, and sin. We want to live as he taught, in order to be united with him now and in the next life.

The **prophets** were good men and women who spoke for God. Sometimes their message was harsh: they asked people to make big changes in their lives and attitudes in order to grow closer to God. At other times, they brought words of comfort.

Saint Paul wrote to the **Colossians**, a Christian community at Colossae in modern-day Turkey, to help them to understand that Jesus Christ is above everything. No powers are greater than Jesus' power.

What is above, that is, in heaven, are those that Jesus teaches: finding the truth, living simply, trusting in God, and caring for those in need. The things of earth distract us from Jesus: being selfish, hurting others, and ignoring the poor.

The **burial cloths** were the fabric that covered the body of a dead person in the tomb. Joseph of Arimathea and Nicodemus made sure that Jesus' body was treated with dignity and buried properly: they covered his face and then wrapped his body with burial cloths.

First Reading *(Acts 2:42-47)*

They devoted themselves to the teaching of the apostles and to the communal life, to the **breaking of bread** and to the prayers. Awe came upon everyone, and many wonders and signs were done through the apostles. All who believed were together and had all things **in common**; they would sell their property and possessions and divide them among all according to each one's need. Every day they devoted themselves to meeting together in the temple area and to breaking bread in their homes. They ate their meals with exultation and sincerity of heart, praising God and enjoying favor with all the people. And every day the Lord added to their number those who were being saved.

The word of the Lord. **Thanks be to God.**

Responsorial Psalm *(Psalm 118:2-4, 13-15, 22-24)*

℟. **Give thanks to the Lord for he is good, his love is everlasting.** *Or* **Alleluia.**

Let the house of Israel say,
    "His mercy endures forever."
Let the house of Aaron say,
    "His mercy endures forever."
Let those who fear the LORD say,
    "His mercy endures forever." ℟.
I was hard pressed and was falling,
    but the LORD helped me.
My strength and my courage is the LORD,
    and he has been my savior.
The joyful shout of victory
    in the tents of the just. ℟.
The stone which the builders rejected
    has become the cornerstone.
By the LORD has this been done;
    it is wonderful in our eyes.
This is the day the LORD has made;
    let us be glad and rejoice in it. ℟.

Second Reading *(1 Peter 1:3-9)*

Blessed be the God and Father of our Lord Jesus Christ, who in his great mercy gave us a new birth to a living hope through the resurrection of Jesus Christ from the dead, to an inheritance that is imperishable, undefiled, and unfading, kept in heaven for you who by the power of God are safeguarded through faith, to a salvation that is ready to be revealed in the final time. In this you **rejoice**, although now for a little while you may have to suffer through various trials, so that the genuineness of your faith, more precious than gold that is perishable even though tested by fire, may prove to be for praise, glory, and honor at the revelation of Jesus Christ. Although you have not seen him you love him; even though you do not see him now yet believe in him, you rejoice with an indescribable and glorious joy, as you attain the goal of your faith, the salvation of your souls.

The word of the Lord. **Thanks be to God.**

Gospel *(John 20:19-31)*

A reading from the holy Gospel according to John.
Glory to you, O Lord.

On the evening of that first day of the week, when the doors were locked, where the disciples were, for fear of the Jews, Jesus came and stood in their midst and said to them, "Peace be with you." When he had said this, he showed them **his hands and his side**. The disciples rejoiced when they saw the Lord. Jesus said to them again, "Peace be with you. As the Father has sent me, so I send you." And when he had said this, he **breathed** on them and said to them, "Receive the Holy Spirit. Whose sins you forgive are forgiven them, and whose sins you retain are retained."

Thomas, called Didymus, one of the Twelve, was not with them when Jesus came. So the other disciples said to him, "We have seen the Lord." But he said to them, "Unless I see the mark of the nails in his hands and put my finger into the nailmarks and put my hand into his side, I will not believe."

Now a week later his disciples were again inside and Thomas was with them. Jesus came, although the doors were locked, and stood in their midst and said, "Peace be with you." Then he said to Thomas, "Put your finger here and see my hands, and bring your hand and put it into my side, and do not be unbelieving, but believe." Thomas answered and said to him, "My Lord and my God!" Jesus said to him, "Have you come to believe because you have seen me? Blessed are those who have not seen and have believed."

Now Jesus did many other signs in the presence of his disciples that are not written in this book. But these are written that you may come to believe that Jesus is the Christ, the Son of God, and that through this belief you may have life in his name.

The Gospel of the Lord. **Praise to you, Lord Jesus Christ.**

Key Words

The apostles gathered for the **breaking of bread**, which means they celebrated the Lord's supper, as we do at every Eucharist or Mass.

In the early Christian community, those who believed in Jesus shared all their belongings **in common**. This way, everyone had all they needed. Today, we can do the same by making sure that no one in our community is in need.

The first Letter of Saint Peter is found in the New Testament. It is a summary of the good news of Jesus and was written to help the early Christians lead faithful lives.

We **rejoice** in our salvation, even when life seems difficult. Jesus conquered death by rising from the dead and we know we will see him when he comes again.

The holy Gospel according to John tells us about the life, death and resurrection of Jesus. It was written about 60 years after Jesus died. Saint John's gospel includes some stories and sayings that are not in the other three gospels (Matthew, Mark and Luke).

By showing **his hands and his side**, Jesus presents the scars left by the nails and the lance that pierced him. It is a way of saying, "It's really me. I was dead, but now I am alive."

When God created the first humans, he **breathed** life into them. Our life comes from the depths of God's being. When Jesus appeared to his disciples after his death, he also breathed on them, filling them with his Spirit.

APRIL 30

3rd Sunday of Easter

First Reading *(Acts 2:14, 22-33)*

Then Peter stood up with the Eleven, raised his voice, and proclaimed: "You who are Jews, indeed all of you staying in Jerusalem. Let this be known to you, and listen to my words. You who are Israelites, hear these words. Jesus the Nazorean was a man commended to you by God with mighty deeds, wonders, and signs, which God worked through him in your midst, as you yourselves know. This man, delivered up by the set plan and foreknowledge of God, you killed, using lawless men to crucify him. But God raised him up, releasing him from the throes of death, because it was impossible for him to be held by it. For David says of him:

> *I saw the Lord ever before me,*
>> *with him at my right hand I shall not be disturbed.*
> *Therefore my heart has been glad and my tongue has exulted;*
>> *my flesh, too, will dwell in hope,*
> *because you will not abandon my soul to the netherworld,*
>> *nor will you suffer your holy one to see corruption.*
> *You have made known to me the paths of life;*
>> *you will fill me with joy in your presence.*

"My brothers, one can confidently say to you about the patriarch **David** that he died and was buried, and his tomb is in our midst to this day. But since he was a prophet and knew that God had sworn an oath to him that he would set one of his descendants upon his throne, he foresaw and spoke of the resurrection of the Christ, that neither was he abandoned to the netherworld nor did his flesh see corruption. God raised this Jesus; of this we are all witnesses. Exalted at the right hand of God, he received the promise of the Holy Spirit from the Father and poured him forth, as you see and hear."

The word of the Lord. **Thanks be to God.**

Responsorial Psalm *(Psalm 16:1-2, 5, 7-8, 9-10, 11)*

R. **Lord, you will show us the path of life.** *Or* **Alleluia.**

> Keep me, O God, for in you I take refuge;
>> I say to the LORD, "My Lord are you."
> O LORD, my allotted portion and my cup,
>> you it is who hold fast my lot. R.

I bless the LORD who counsels me;
    even in the night my heart exhorts me.
I set the LORD ever before me;
    with him at my right hand I shall not be disturbed. R.
Therefore my heart is glad and my soul rejoices,
    my body, too, abides in confidence;
because you will not abandon my soul
      to the netherworld,
    nor will you suffer your faithful one
      to undergo corruption. R.
You will show me the path to life,
    abounding joy in your presence,
    the delights at your right hand forever. R.

Second Reading *(1 Peter 1:17-21)*

Beloved: If you invoke as Father him who judges impartially according to each one's works, conduct yourselves with **reverence** during the time of your sojourning, realizing that you were ransomed from your futile conduct, handed on by your ancestors, not with perishable things like silver or gold but with the precious blood of Christ as of a spotless unblemished **lamb**.

He was known before the foundation of the world but revealed in the final time for you, who through him believe in God who raised him from the dead and gave him glory, so that your faith and hope are in God.

The word of the Lord. **Thanks be to God.**

Gospel *(Luke 24:13-35)*

A reading from the holy Gospel according to Luke.
Glory to you, O Lord.

That very day, the first day of the week, two of Jesus' disciples were going to a village seven miles from Jerusalem called Emmaus, and they were conversing about all the things that had occurred. And it happened that while they were conversing and debating, Jesus himself drew near and walked with them, but their eyes were prevented from recognizing him. He asked them, "What are you discussing as you walk along?" They stopped, looking downcast. One of them, named Cleopas, said to him in reply, "Are you the only visitor to Jerusalem who does not know of the things that have taken place there in these days?" And he replied to them, "What sort of things?" They said to him, "The things that happened to Jesus the Nazarene, who was a prophet mighty in deed and word before God and all the people, how our chief priests and rulers both handed him over to a sentence of death and crucified him. But we were hoping that he would be the one to redeem Israel; and besides all this, it is now the third day since this took place. Some women from our group, however, have astounded us: they were at the tomb early in the morning and did not find his body; they came back and reported that they had indeed seen a vision of angels who announced that he was alive. Then some of those with us went to the tomb and found things just as the women had described, but him they did not see." And he said to them, "Oh, how foolish you are! How slow of heart to believe all that the prophets spoke! Was it not necessary that the Christ should suffer these things and enter into his glory?" Then beginning with Moses and all the prophets, he interpreted to them what referred to him in all the **Scriptures**. As they approached the village to which they were going, he gave the impression that he was going on farther. But they urged him, "Stay with us, for it is nearly evening and the day is almost over." So he went in to stay with them. And it happened that, while he was with them at table, he took bread, said the blessing, broke it, and gave it to them. With that their eyes were opened and they recognized him, but he vanished from their sight. Then they said to each other, "Were not our hearts burning within us while he spoke to us on the way and opened the Scriptures to us?" So they set out at once and returned to Jerusalem where they found gathered together the eleven and those with them who were saying, "The Lord has truly been raised and has appeared to Simon!" Then the two recounted what had taken place on the way and how he was made known to them in the **breaking of bread**.

The Gospel of the Lord. **Praise to you, Lord Jesus Christ.**

David was the second king of Israel. He lived about 1,000 years before Christ. David is considered to be the author of the 150 psalms. In this passage from the Acts of the Apostles, Saint Peter is quoting from Psalm 16.

If we have **reverence** for someone, we are filled with awe because of their greatness and we try to honor them with our lives.

Jewish people made sacrifices of animals to God. Because Jesus' sacrifice brought us back to God, the Bible compares Jesus to a **lamb**, one without any stain.

The holy Gospel according to Luke is one of the four gospels in the New Testament or Christian Scriptures. It was written for people who, like Saint Luke, weren't Jewish before becoming Christian.

The **Scriptures** are the written word of God. We read them in the Bible, both the Hebrew Scriptures (Old Testament) and the Christian Scriptures (New Testament).

Jesus' disciples recognized him in the **breaking of bread**, because Jesus had done the same thing at many meals, especially the Last Supper. Jesus said to do this in his memory, and we remember Jesus as our living bread when we celebrate the Eucharist.

MAY 7

4th Sunday of Easter

First Reading *(Acts 2:14a, 36-41)*

Then Peter stood up with **the Eleven**, raised his voice, and proclaimed: "Let the whole house of Israel know for certain that God has made both Lord and Christ, this Jesus whom you crucified."

Now when they heard this, they were cut to the heart, and they asked Peter and the other apostles, "What are we to do, my brothers?" Peter said to them, "**Repent** and be baptized, every one of you, in the name of Jesus Christ for the forgiveness of your sins; and you will receive the gift of the Holy Spirit. For the promise is made to you and to your children and to all those far off, **whomever the Lord our God will call.**" He testified with many other arguments, and was exhorting them, "Save yourselves from this corrupt generation." Those who accepted his message were baptized, and about three thousand persons were added that day.

The word of the Lord. **Thanks be to God.**

Responsorial Psalm *(Psalm 23:1-3a, 3b-4, 5, 6)*

℞. **The Lord is my shepherd; there is nothing I shall want.** *Or* **Alleluia.**

The LORD is my **shepherd**; I shall not want.
　　In verdant pastures he gives me repose;
beside restful waters he leads me;
　　he refreshes my soul. ℞.
He guides me in right paths
　　for his name's sake.
Even though I walk in the dark valley
　　I fear no evil; for you are at my side
with your rod and your staff
　　that give me courage. ℞.
You spread the table before me
　　in the sight of my foes;
you anoint my head with oil;
　　my cup overflows. ℞.
Only goodness and kindness follow me
　　all the days of my life;
and I shall dwell in the house of the LORD
　　for years to come. ℞.

Second Reading *(1 Peter 2:20b-25)*

Beloved: If you are patient when you suffer for doing what is good, this is a grace before God. For to this you have been called, because Christ also suffered for you, leaving you an example that you should follow in his footsteps. *He committed no sin, and no deceit was found in his mouth.*

When he was insulted, he returned no insult; when he suffered, he did not threaten; instead, he handed himself over to the one who judges justly. He himself bore our sins in his body upon the cross, so that, free from sin, we might live for righteousness. By his wounds you have been healed. For you had gone astray like sheep, but you have now returned to the shepherd and guardian of your souls.

The word of the Lord. **Thanks be to God.**

Gospel *(John 10:1-10)*

A reading from the holy Gospel according to John.
Glory to you, O Lord.

Jesus said: "Amen, amen, I say to you, whoever does not enter a **sheepfold** through the gate but climbs over elsewhere is a thief and a robber. But whoever enters through the gate is the shepherd of the sheep. The gatekeeper opens it for him, and the sheep hear his voice, as the shepherd calls his own sheep by name and leads them out. When he has driven out all his own, he walks ahead of them, and the sheep follow him, because they recognize his voice. But they will not follow a stranger; they will run away from him, because they do not recognize the voice of strangers." Although Jesus used this figure of speech, the Pharisees did not realize what he was trying to tell them.

So Jesus said again, "Amen, amen, I say to you, I am the gate for the sheep. All who came before me are thieves and robbers, but the sheep did not listen to them. I am the gate. Whoever enters through me will be saved, and will come in and go out and find pasture. A thief comes only to steal and slaughter and destroy; I came so that they might have life and have it more **abundantly**."

The Gospel of the Lord. **Praise to you, Lord Jesus Christ.**

Key Words

The Eleven mentioned in the Acts of the Apostles are the disciples of Jesus. They were twelve at first, but Judas Iscariot, who betrayed Jesus, left before Jesus died.

To **repent** means to be sorry for doing something wrong and to change our behavior for the better.

When Saint Peter says that God's promises are for **whomever the Lord God will call**, he is saying something new. He means that God's promises are not just for the People of Israel, but for all people everywhere. This is the New Covenant.

A **shepherd** is someone who takes care of a flock of sheep. He would spend days or weeks with his flock, sleeping with them and making sure they were always safe. God loves us with the same constant care.

The **sheepfold** is a fenced-in area for sheep. It helps keep the sheep safe from other animals that might attack them.

When we have life **abundantly**, it means our hearts are full of joy and peace. We live our lives wanting to help others because of our friendship with Jesus.

First Reading *(Acts 6:1-7)*

As the number of disciples continued to grow, the Hellenists complained against the Hebrews because their widows were being neglected in the daily distribution. So the Twelve called together the community of the disciples and said, "It is not right for us to neglect the **word of God** to serve at table. Brothers, select from among you seven reputable men, filled with the Spirit and wisdom, whom we shall appoint to this task, whereas we shall devote ourselves to prayer and to the ministry of the word." The proposal was acceptable to the whole community, so they chose **Stephen**, a man filled with faith and the Holy Spirit, also Philip, Prochorus, Nicanor, Timon, Parmenas, and Nicholas of Antioch, a convert to Judaism. They presented these men to the apostles who prayed and **laid hands** on them. The word of God continued to spread, and the number of the disciples in Jerusalem increased greatly; even a large group of priests were becoming obedient to the faith.

The word of the Lord. **Thanks be to God.**

Responsorial Psalm *(Psalm 33:1-2, 4-5, 18-19)*

R. **Lord, let your mercy be on us, as we place our trust in you.** *Or* **Alleluia.**

Exult, you just, in the LORD;
    praise from the upright is fitting.
Give thanks to the LORD on the harp;
    with the ten-stringed lyre chant his praises. R.
Upright is the word of the LORD,
    and all his works are trustworthy.
He loves justice and right;
    of the kindness of the LORD the earth is full. R.
See, the eyes of the LORD are upon those who fear him,
    upon those who hope for his kindness,
To deliver them from death
    and preserve them in spite of famine. R.

Second Reading (1 Peter 2:4-9)

Beloved: Come to him, a living stone, rejected by human beings but chosen and precious in the sight of God, and, like **living stones**, let yourselves be built into a spiritual house to be a **holy priesthood** to offer spiritual sacrifices acceptable to God through Jesus Christ. For it says in Scripture:

> *Behold, I am laying a stone in Zion,*
> *a cornerstone, chosen and precious,*
> *and whoever believes in it shall not be put to shame.*

Therefore, its value is for you who have faith, but for those without faith:

> *The stone that the builders rejected*
> *has become the cornerstone,*

and

> *A stone that will make people stumble,*
> *and a rock that will make them fall.*

They stumble by disobeying the word, as is their destiny.

You are "a chosen race, a royal priesthood, a holy nation, a people of his own, so that you may announce the praises" of him who called you out of darkness into his wonderful light.

The word of the Lord. **Thanks be to God.**

Gospel (John 14:1-12)

A reading from the holy Gospel according to John.
Glory to you, O Lord.

Jesus said to his disciples: "Do not let your hearts be troubled. You have faith in God; have faith also in me. In my Father's house there are many dwelling places. If there were not, would I have told you that I am going to prepare a place for you? And if I go and prepare a place for you, I will come back again and **take you to myself**, so that where I am you also may be. Where I am going you know the way." Thomas said to him, "Master, we do not know where you are going; how can we know the way?" Jesus said to him, "I am the way and the truth and the life. No one comes to the Father except through me. If you know me, then you will also know my Father. From now on you do know him and have seen him." Philip said to him, "Master, show us the Father, and that will be enough for us." Jesus said to him, "Have I been with you for so long a time and you still do not know me, Philip? Whoever has seen me has seen the Father. How can you say, 'Show us the

Father'? Do you not believe that I am in the Father and the Father is in me? The words that I speak to you I do not speak on my own. The Father who dwells in me is doing his works. Believe me that I am in the Father and the Father is in me, or else, believe because of the works themselves. Amen, amen, I say to you, whoever believes in me will do the works that I do, and will do greater ones than these, because I am going to the Father."

The Gospel of the Lord. **Praise to you, Lord Jesus Christ.**

Key Words

The **word of God** is the good news—that Jesus is the Savior of the world! The disciples were worried that they were so busy trying to help everybody and spending less and less time sharing the good news. So they named some people to help serve the needs of the poor.

Stephen was one of the first ministers in the early Church. He did much good work. Stephen was killed because of his faith in Jesus and was the first martyr. The feast of Saint Stephen is on December 26.

The disciples **laid hands** on the heads of others as a form of prayer. It was also a way of sending someone off to do a task. This gesture is now part of certain sacraments, such as confirmation and holy orders (priesthood). It is a sign that the power of God, the Holy Spirit, is being given to the person.

When Saint Peter calls us **living stones**, he is telling us that we are a very important part of the Church. If we do not all stand together, the Church will lose its strength.

Through our baptism, all Christians share in the **holy priesthood** of Jesus: we offer our lives to God and rejoice in his love. Priests are anointed as part of a special sacrament to preside at Eucharist and some of the other sacraments, and to be leaders of the community.

When Jesus says that he will "**take you to myself**," he is making a beautiful promise. Jesus will take us into his heart.

163

First Reading *(Acts 8:5-8, 14-17)*

Philip went down to the city of Samaria and proclaimed the Christ to them. With one accord, the crowds paid attention to what was said by Philip when they heard it and saw the signs he was doing. For unclean spirits, crying out in a loud voice, came out of many possessed people, and many paralyzed or crippled people were cured. There was great joy in that city.

Now when the apostles in Jerusalem heard that Samaria had accepted the word of God, they sent them Peter and John, who went down and prayed for them, that they might receive the **Holy Spirit**, for it had not yet fallen upon any of them; they had only been baptized in the name of the Lord Jesus. Then they laid hands on them and they received the Holy Spirit.

The word of the Lord. **Thanks be to God.**

Responsorial Psalm *(Psalm 66:1-3, 4-5, 6-7, 16, 20)*

R. **Let all the earth cry out to God with joy.** Or **Alleluia.**

Shout joyfully to God, all the earth,
   sing praise to the glory of his name;
   proclaim his glorious praise.
Say to God, "How tremendous are your deeds!" R.
"Let all on earth worship and sing praise to you,
   sing praise to your name!"
Come and see the works of God,
   his tremendous deeds among
      the children of Adam. R.
He has changed the sea into dry land;
   through the river they passed on foot;
   therefore let us rejoice in him.
He rules by his might forever. R.
Hear now, all you who fear God, while I declare
   what he has done for me.
Blessed be God who refused me not
   my prayer or his kindness! R.

Second Reading *(1 Peter 3:15-18)*

Beloved: **Sanctify** Christ as Lord in your hearts. Always be ready to give an explanation to anyone who asks you for a reason for your hope, but do it with gentleness and reverence, keeping your conscience clear, so that, when you are maligned, those who defame your good conduct in Christ may themselves be put to shame. For it is better to suffer for doing good, if that be the will of God, than for doing evil. For **Christ** also suffered for sins once, the righteous for the sake of the unrighteous, that he might lead you to God. Put to death in the flesh, he was brought to life in the Spirit.

The word of the Lord. **Thanks be to God.**

Gospel *(John 14:15-21)*

A reading from the holy Gospel according to John.
Glory to you, O Lord.

Jesus said to his disciples: "If you love me, you will keep my commandments. And I will ask the Father, and he will give you another **Advocate** to be with you always, the Spirit of truth, whom the world cannot accept, because it neither sees nor knows him. But you know him, because he **remains with** you, and will be in you. I will not leave you orphans; I will come to you. In a little while the world will no longer see me, but you will see me, because I live and you will live. On that day you will realize that I am in my Father and you are in me and I in you. Whoever has my commandments and observes them is **the one who loves me**. And whoever loves me will be loved by my Father, and I will love him and reveal myself to him."

The Gospel of the Lord. **Praise to you, Lord Jesus Christ.**

Philip in today's reading from the Acts of the Apostles is not Philip the apostle, but one of the seven deacons named by the apostles to care for widows and the poor. He was mentioned last Sunday, along with Saint Stephen, the first martyr.

Before Jesus went to heaven, he said not to be afraid, because he would send the **Holy Spirit** to help us remember all that Jesus taught. The Holy Spirit came upon the early Church at Pentecost.

To **sanctify** something is to make it holy. When we carry the Holy Spirit in our hearts, and try to love each other, we proclaim that Jesus is holy and sanctify Jesus.

Christ is a Greek word that means "anointed." The chosen person was blessed with holy oil and given a special mission. The Aramaic word for "anointed" is "Messiah."

The **Advocate** is another name for the Holy Spirit, sent by Jesus to be our helper and guide until the end of time.

The Holy Spirit **remains with** or lives in us. The Spirit encourages us and gives us the words we need to speak about our faith in Jesus Christ.

When Jesus speaks of "**the one who loves me**," he means those who show their love of God by their loving actions. Love is more than a good feeling—it is as way of life.

MAY 28

Ascension of the Lord
or Seventh Sunday of Easter

If your diocese celebrates the Ascension of the Lord on Thursday, May 25, then this Sunday is the Seventh Sunday of Easter. The readings for the Seventh Sunday of Easter can be found on page 171.

First Reading (*Acts 1:1-11*)

In the first book, **Theophilus**, I dealt with all that Jesus did and taught until the day he was taken up, after giving instructions through the Holy Spirit to the apostles whom he had chosen. He presented himself alive to them by many proofs after he had suffered, appearing to them during forty days and speaking about the kingdom of God. While meeting with them, he enjoined them not to depart from Jerusalem, but to wait for "the promise of the Father about which you have heard me speak; for John baptized with water, but in a few days you will be baptized with the Holy Spirit."

When they had gathered together they asked him, "Lord, are you at this time going to restore the **kingdom** to Israel?" He answered them, "It is not for you to know the times or seasons that the Father has established by his own authority. But you will receive power when the Holy Spirit comes upon you, and you will be my witnesses in Jerusalem, throughout Judea and Samaria, and to the ends of the earth." When he had said this, as they were looking on, he was lifted up, and a cloud took him from their sight. While they were looking intently at the sky as he was going, suddenly two men dressed in white garments stood beside them. They said, "Men of **Galilee**, why are you standing there looking at the sky? This Jesus who has been taken up from you into heaven will return in the same way you have seen him going into heaven."

The word of the Lord. **Thanks be to God.**

Responsorial Psalm (*Psalm 47:2-3, 6-7, 8-9*)

R. **God mounts his throne to shouts of joy: a blare of trumpets for the Lord.** Or **Alleluia.**

All you peoples, clap your hands,
    shout to God with cries of gladness,
for the LORD, the Most High, the awesome,
    is the great king over all the earth. R.
God mounts his throne amid shouts of joy;
    the LORD, amid trumpet blasts.
Sing praise to God, sing praise;
    sing praise to our king, sing praise. R.

R. **God mounts his throne to shouts of joy: a blare of trumpets for the Lord.** *Or* **Alleluia.**

For king of all the earth is God;
    sing hymns of praise.
God reigns over the nations,
    God sits upon his holy throne. R.

Second Reading *(Ephesians 1:17-23)*

Brothers and sisters: May the God of our Lord Jesus Christ, the Father of glory, give you a Spirit of wisdom and revelation resulting in knowledge of him. May the eyes of your hearts be enlightened, that you may know what is the hope that belongs to his call, what are the riches of glory in his inheritance among the holy ones, and what is the surpassing greatness of his power for us who believe, in accord with the exercise of his great might: which he worked in Christ, raising him from the dead and seating him at his **right hand** in the heavens, far above every **principality, authority, power, and dominion**, and every name that is named not only in this age but also in the one to come. And he put all things beneath his feet and gave him as head over all things to the church, which is his body, the fullness of the one who fills all things in every way.

The word of the Lord. **Thanks be to God.**

Gospel *(Matthew 28:16-20)*

A reading from the holy Gospel according to Matthew.
Glory to you, O Lord.

The eleven disciples went to Galilee, to the mountain to which Jesus had ordered them. When they saw him, they worshiped, but they doubted. Then Jesus approached and said to them, "All power in heaven and on earth has been given to me. Go, therefore, and make disciples of all nations, baptizing them in the name of the Father, and of the Son, and of the Holy Spirit, teaching them to observe all that I have commanded you. And behold, **I am with you always**, until the end of the age."

First Reading *(Acts 1:12-14)*

After Jesus had been taken up to heaven the apostles returned to Jerusalem from the mount called Olivet, which is near Jerusalem, a sabbath day's journey away.

When they entered the city they went to the upper room where they were staying, Peter and John and James and Andrew, Philip and Thomas, Bartholomew and Matthew, James son of Alphaeus, Simon the Zealot, and Judas son of James. All these devoted themselves with one accord to prayer, together with some women, and Mary the mother of Jesus, and his brothers.

The word of the Lord. **Thanks be to God.**

Responsorial Psalm *(Psalm 27:1, 4, 7-8)*

R̰. **I believe that I shall see the good things of the Lord in the land of the living.** Or **Alleluia.**

The LORD is my light and my salvation;
    whom should I fear?
The LORD is my life's refuge;
    of whom should I be afraid? R̰.
One thing I ask of the LORD;
    this I seek:
To dwell in the house of the LORD
    all the days of my life,
that I may gaze on the loveliness of the LORD
    and contemplate his temple. R̰.
Hear, O LORD, the sound of my call;
    have pity on me, and answer me.
Of you my heart speaks; you my glance seeks. R̰.

Second Reading *(1 Peter 4:13-16)*

Beloved: Rejoice to the extent that you share in the sufferings of Christ, so that when his glory is revealed you may also rejoice exultantly. If you are insulted for the name of Christ, blessed are you, for the Spirit of glory and of God rests upon you. But let no one among you be made to suffer as a murderer, a thief, an evildoer, or as an intriguer. But whoever is made to suffer as a Christian should not be ashamed but glorify God because of the name.

The word of the Lord. **Thanks be to God.**

Gospel *(John 17:1-11a)*

A reading from the holy Gospel according to John.
Glory to you, O Lord.

Jesus raised his eyes to heaven and said, "Father, the hour has come. Give glory to your son, so that your son may glorify you, just as you gave him authority over all people, so that your son may give eternal life to all you gave him. Now this is eternal life, that they should know you, the only true God, and the one whom you sent, Jesus Christ. I glorified you on earth by accomplishing the work that you gave me to do. Now glorify me, Father, with you, with the glory that I had with you before the world began.

"I revealed your name to those whom you gave me out of the world. They belonged to you, and you gave them to me, and they have kept your word. Now they know that everything you gave me is from you, because the words you gave to me I have given to them, and they accepted them and truly understood that I came from you, and they have believed that you sent me. I pray for them. I do not pray for the world but for the ones you have given me, because they are yours, and everything of mine is yours and everything of yours is mine, and I have been glorified in them. And now I will no longer be in the world, but they are in the world, while I am coming to you."

The Gospel of the Lord. **Praise to you, Lord Jesus Christ.**

Key Words

On the feast of the **Ascension**, we remember the moment when Jesus returned to the house of his Father, forty days after rising from the dead. Jesus no longer appeared to his disciples, but he sent the Holy Spirit at Pentecost.

Theophilus (a Greek name that means "friend of God") lived in Antioch. He was a leader of the Christian communities of Greece. Saint Luke sent his gospel as well as the Acts of the Apostles to him.

In the days of Jesus, Israel was part of the Roman Empire and was not free to govern itself. Some of the disciples hoped that Jesus would free Israel from Rome's bitter rule and bring back the ancient **kingdom** of Israel.

Galilee is a province in the north of Israel. Nazareth, the town where Jesus lived with his parents, is in Galilee. So is the Sea of Tiberias, where some of Jesus' disciples worked as fishermen. In Jerusalem, to the south, Jesus and his followers were recognized as Galileans because of their accent.

When Saint Paul says that Jesus sits at the **right hand** of God, he is saying that Jesus is as close as possible to God the Father. There is no place closer to God.

When Saint Paul speaks of all **principality, authority, power, and dominion**, he is not talking about earthly governments. Instead, he means different kinds of angels in heaven. Jesus sits so close to the Father in heaven that he is above all the angels.

"**I am with you always**" is the promise Jesus made to the disciples and to us. He is with us when we gather in his name as a community, when we listen to God's word, when we celebrate the Eucharist, and when we share his love with others.

JUNE 4
Pentecost Sunday

First Reading (Acts 2:1-11)

When the time for Pentecost was fulfilled, they were all in one place together. And suddenly there came from the sky a noise like a strong driving wind, and it filled the entire house in which they were. Then there appeared to them tongues as of fire, which parted and came to rest on each one of them. And they were all filled with the Holy Spirit and began to speak in different tongues, as the Spirit enabled them to proclaim.

Now there were devout Jews from every nation under heaven staying in Jerusalem. At this sound, they gathered in a large crowd, but they were confused because each one heard them speaking in his own language. They were astounded, and in amazement they asked, "Are not all these people who are speaking Galileans? Then how does each of us hear them in his native language? We are Parthians, Medes, and Elamites, inhabitants of Mesopotamia, Judea and Cappadocia, Pontus and Asia, Phrygia and Pamphylia, Egypt and the districts of Libya near Cyrene, as well as travelers from Rome, both Jews and converts to Judaism, Cretans and Arabs, yet we hear them speaking in our own tongues of the mighty acts of God."

The word of the Lord. **Thanks be to God.**

Responsorial Psalm (Psalm 104:1, 24, 29-30, 31, 34)

R. **Lord, send out your Spirit, and renew the face of the earth.** Or **Alleluia.**

Bless the Lord, O my soul!
O Lord, my God, you are great indeed!
How manifold are your works, O Lord!
The earth is full of your creatures. R.
If you take away their breath, they perish
and return to their dust.
When you send forth your spirit, they are created,
and you renew the face of the earth. R.
May the glory of the Lord endure forever;
may the Lord be glad in his works!
Pleasing to him be my theme;
I will be glad in the Lord. R.

175

Second Reading *(1 Corinthians 12:3b-7, 12-13)*

Brothers and sisters: No one can say, "Jesus is Lord," except by the Holy Spirit.

There are different kinds of spiritual gifts but the same Spirit; there are different forms of service but the same Lord; there are different workings but the same God who produces all of them in everyone. To each individual the manifestation of the Spirit is given for **some benefit**.

As a **body** is one though it has many parts, and all the parts of the body, though many, are one body, so also Christ. For in one Spirit we were all baptized into one body, whether Jews or Greeks, slaves or free persons, and we were all given to drink of one Spirit.

The word of the Lord. **Thanks be to God.**

Sequence *(Veni, Sancte Spiritus)*

Come, Holy Spirit, come!
And from your celestial home
   Shed a ray of light divine!
Come, Father of the poor!
Come, source of all our store!
   Come, within our bosoms shine.
You, of comforters the best;
You, the soul's most welcome guest;
   Sweet refreshment here below.
In our labor, rest most sweet;
Grateful coolness in the heat;
   Solace in the midst of woe.
O most blessed Light divine,
Shine within these hearts of yours,
   And our inmost being fill!
Where you are not, we have naught,
Nothing good in deed or thought,
   Nothing free from taint of ill.
Heal our wounds, our strength renew;
On our dryness pour your dew;

Wash the stains of guilt away.
Bend the stubborn heart and will;
Melt the frozen, warm the chill;
    Guide the steps that go astray.
On the faithful, who adore
And confess you, evermore
    In your sevenfold gift descend.
Give them virtue's sure reward;
Give them your salvation, Lord;
    Give them joys that never end. Amen.
    Alleluia.

Gospel *(John 20:19-23)*

A reading from the holy Gospel according to John.
Glory to you, O Lord.

On the evening of that first day of the week, when the doors were locked, where the disciples were, for fear of the Jews, Jesus came and stood in their midst and said to them, "**Peace be with you**." When he had said this, he showed them his hands and his side. The disciples rejoiced when they saw the Lord. Jesus said to them again, "Peace be with you. As the Father has sent me, so I send you." And when he had said this, he breathed on them and said to them, "**Receive the Holy Spirit**. Whose sins you forgive are forgiven them, and whose sins you retain are retained."

The Gospel of the Lord. **Praise to you, Lord Jesus Christ.**

God's **mighty acts** are so great that they cannot be counted, but the greatest of these is that he sent his Son to save us. The disciples proclaimed the good news of God's marvelous deed—the death and resurrection of Jesus.

The **Corinthians** were a community of Christians who lived in Corinth, a city in Greece. Saint Paul wrote them several letters, two of which were preserved and are in the Bible.

Each of us is unique and has received our own gifts through the Holy Spirit. But we must not keep these gifts to ourselves: they are for **some benefit**, for the good of everyone in the community.

Saint Paul compares the Church to a human **body**. Although all the parts are different, each is important and all the parts together make one complete body.

When Jesus appears to his disciples after the resurrection, he often says, "**Peace be with you**." The disciples are afraid and confused, and Jesus tells them not to worry and to be at peace. We can turn to Jesus when we are frightened and confused and we will know his peace in our hearts.

Jesus says to his disciples, "**Receive the Holy Spirit,**" and he gives them an important power—to forgive sins in God's name. As Christians we care a lot about forgiveness. Jesus taught us to forgive each other when he gave us the Our Father prayer ("as we forgive those who trespass against us").

First Reading *(Exodus 34:4b-6, 8-9)*

Early in the morning Moses went up **Mount Sinai** as the LORD had commanded him, taking along the **two stone tablets**.

Having come down in a cloud, the LORD stood with Moses there and proclaimed his name, "LORD." Thus the LORD passed before him and cried out, "The LORD, the LORD, a merciful and gracious God, slow to anger and rich in kindness and fidelity." Moses at once bowed down to the ground in worship. Then he said, "If I find favor with you, O LORD, do come along in our company. This is indeed a stiff-necked people; yet pardon our wickedness and sins, and receive us as your own."

The word of the Lord. **Thanks be to God.**

Responsorial Canticle *(Daniel 3:52, 53, 54, 55)*

R. **Glory and praise for ever!**

Blessed are you, O LORD, the God of our fathers,
 praiseworthy and exalted above all forever;
And blessed is your holy and glorious name,
 praiseworthy and exalted above all for all ages. R.
Blessed are you in the temple of your holy glory,
 praiseworthy and glorious above all forever. R.
Blessed are you on the throne of your kingdom,
 praiseworthy and exalted above all forever. R.
Blessed are you who look into the depths
 from your throne upon the cherubim,
 praiseworthy and exalted above all forever. R.

Second Reading *(2 Corinthians 13:11-13)*

Brothers and sisters, rejoice. Mend your ways, encourage one another, agree with one another, live in peace, and the God of love and peace will be with you. Greet one another with a holy kiss. All the holy ones greet you.

The grace of the Lord Jesus Christ and the love of God and the fellowship of the Holy Spirit be with all of you.

The word of the Lord. **Thanks be to God.**

Gospel *(John 3:16-18)*
A reading from the holy Gospel according to John.
Glory to you, O Lord.

God so loved the world that he gave his only Son, so that everyone who believes in him might not **perish** but might have eternal life. For God did not send his Son into the world to condemn the world, but that the world might be saved through him. Whoever believes in him will not be condemned, but whoever does not believe has already been condemned, because he has not believed in the name of the only Son of God.

The Gospel of the Lord. **Praise to you, Lord Jesus Christ.**

The **Trinity** is the teaching of three persons in one God: the Father, the Son, and the Holy Spirit. Today, on Trinity Sunday, we celebrate this mystery.

The second book of the Bible is called **Exodus**. It is an important book because it tells how God liberated his people from slavery in Egypt, made a covenant with them and gave them the Ten Commandments, which taught them how to live correctly.

Mount Sinai is a place where God often visited his people. God spoke to Moses on Mount Sinai and gave him the Ten Commandments. Mount Sinai was also called Mount Horeb.

Even today we might inscribe important things in stone. We do this so that the words will not be erased or forgotten. When God spoke to Moses on Mount Sinai, God ordered him to write the Ten Commandments on **two stone tablets**.

Saying "**Blessed are you, O Lord**" is a way of praising God.

We are saying, "Let the whole world know how great and wonderful God is!"

To **perish** is to die. Jesus promises that those who believe in him will not perish forever. Jesus promises us eternal life with God, and even though we will die, we already enjoy our new life with God.

JUNE 18
Solemnity of the Most Holy Body and Blood of Christ

First Reading *(Deuteronomy 8:2-3, 14b-16a)*

Moses said to the people: "Remember how for forty years now the LORD, your God, has directed all your journeying in the desert, so as to test you by affliction and find out whether or not it was your intention to keep his **commandments**. He therefore let you be afflicted with hunger, and then fed you with **manna**, a food unknown to you and your fathers, in order to show you that not by bread alone does one live, but by every word that comes forth from the mouth of the LORD.

"Do not forget the LORD, your God, who brought you out of the land of Egypt, that place of slavery; who guided you through the vast and terrible desert with its saraph serpents and scorpions, its parched and waterless ground; who brought forth water for you from the flinty rock and fed you in the desert with manna, a food unknown to your fathers."

The word of the Lord. **Thanks be to God.**

Responsorial Psalm *(Psalm 147:12-13, 14-15, 19-20)*

R. **Praise the Lord, Jerusalem.** *Or* **Alleluia!**

Glorify the LORD, O Jerusalem;
    praise your God, O Zion.
For he has strengthened the bars of your gates;
    he has blessed your children within you. R.
He has granted peace in your borders;
    with the best of wheat he fills you.
He sends forth his command to the earth;
    swiftly runs his word! R.
He has proclaimed his word to Jacob,
    his statutes and his ordinances to Israel.
He has not done thus for any other nation;
    his ordinances he has not made known to them.
        Alleluia. R.

Second Reading *(1 Corinthians 10:16-17)*

Brothers and sisters: The cup of blessing that we bless, is it not a participation in the blood of Christ? The bread that we break, is it not a participation in the body of Christ? Because the loaf of bread is one, we, though many, are one body, for we all partake of the one loaf.

The word of the Lord. **Thanks be to God.**

Sequence *(Optional)*

The shorter version begins at the asterisks.

Laud, O Zion, your salvation,
Laud with hymns of exultation,
    Christ, your king and shepherd true:

Bring him all the praise you know,
He is more than you bestow.
    Never can you reach his due.

Special theme for glad thanksgiving
Is the quick'ning and the living
    Bread today before you set:

From his hands of old partaken,
As we know, by faith unshaken,
    Where the Twelve at supper met.

Full and clear ring out your chanting,
Joy nor sweetest grace be wanting,
    From your heart let praises burst:

For today the feast is holden,
When the institution olden
    Of that supper was rehearsed.

Here the new law's new oblation,
By the new king's revelation,
    Ends the form of ancient rite:

Now the new the old effaces,
Truth away the shadow chases,
    Light dispels the gloom of night.

What he did at supper seated,
Christ ordained to be repeated,
    His memorial ne'er to cease:

And his rule for guidance taking,
Bread and wine we hallow, making
    Thus our sacrifice of peace.

This the truth each Christian learns,
Bread into his flesh he turns,
   To his precious blood the wine:

Sight has fail'd, nor thought conceives,
But a dauntless faith believes,
   Resting on a pow'r divine.

Here beneath these signs are hidden
Priceless things to sense forbidden;
   Sign, not things are all we see:

Blood is poured and flesh is broken,
Yet in either wondrous token
   Christ entire we know to be.

Whoso of this food partakes,
Does not rend the Lord nor breaks;
   Christ is whole to all that tastes:

Thousands are, as one, receivers,
One, as thousands of believers,
   Eats of him who cannot waste.

Bad and good the feast are sharing,
Of what divers dooms preparing,
   Endless death, or endless life.

Life to these, to those damnation,
See how like participation
   Is with unlike issues rife.

When the sacrament is broken,
Doubt not, but believe 'tis spoken,
   That each sever'd outward token
     doth the very whole contain.

Nought the precious gift divides,
Breaking but the sign betides
   Jesus still the same abides,
     still unbroken does remain.

*   *   *

The shorter form of the sequence begins here.

Lo! the angel's food is given
To the pilgrim who has striven;
    See the children's bread from heaven,
      which on dogs may not be spent.

Truth the ancient types fulfilling,
Isaac bound, a victim willing,
    Paschal lamb, its lifeblood spilling,
    manna to the fathers sent.

Very bread, good shepherd, tend us,
Jesu, of your love befriend us,
    You refresh us, you defend us,
    Your eternal goodness send us
In the land of life to see.

You who all things can and know,
Who on earth such food bestow,
    Grant us with your saints, though lowest,
    Where the heav'nly feast you show,
Fellow heirs and guests to be. Amen. Alleluia.

Gospel *(John 6:51-58)*

A reading from the holy Gospel according to John.
Glory to you, O Lord.

Jesus said to the Jewish crowds: "I am the living bread that came
down from heaven; whoever eats this bread will live forever; and
the bread that I will give is my flesh for the life of the world."
    The Jews quarreled among themselves, saying, "How can this
man give us his flesh to eat?" Jesus said to them, "Amen, amen, I
say to you, unless you eat the flesh of the Son of Man and drink
his blood, you do not have life within you. Whoever eats my flesh
and drinks my blood has eternal life, and I will raise him on the
last day. For my flesh is true food, and my blood is true drink.
Whoever eats my flesh and drinks my blood remains in me and I
in him. Just as the living Father sent me and I have life because of
the Father, so also the one who feeds on me will have life because
of me. This is the bread that came down from heaven. Unlike
your **ancestors** who ate and still died, whoever eats this bread
will live forever."

The Gospel of the Lord. **Praise to you, Lord Jesus Christ.**

Key Words

God gave his **commandments** to Moses and God's people on Mount Sinai. They help us to love God and all the people we meet along the road of life.

Manna is a food that God sent to the Israelites when they fled from Egypt. They were crossing the desert and had nothing to eat. After Moses asked God for help, the people woke up the next morning and found manna on the ground. Manna was like bread falling from heaven.

The holy Gospel according to John tells us about the life, death, and resurrection of Jesus. It was written about 60 years after Jesus died. Saint John's gospel includes some stories and sayings that are not in the other three gospels (Matthew, Mark and Luke).

The people who lived before us, our **ancestors**, left slavery in Egypt 1,000 years before Christ was born. They wandered in the desert for forty years before coming to the Promised Land. When they were hungry, God sent them manna from heaven. God sent his son, Jesus, to be our living bread. God always takes care of his people!

JUNE 25

12th Sunday in Ordinary Time

First Reading *(Jeremiah 20:10-13)*

Jeremiah said:
"I hear the whisperings of many:
      'Terror on every side!
      Denounce! Let us denounce him!'
All those who were my friends
      are on the watch for any misstep of mine.
'Perhaps he will be trapped; then we can prevail,
      and take our vengeance on him.'
But the LORD is with me, like a mighty champion:
      my persecutors will stumble, they will not triumph.
In their failure they will be put to utter shame,
      to lasting, unforgettable confusion.
O LORD of hosts, you who test the just,
      who probe mind and heart,
let me witness the vengeance you take on them,
      for to you I have entrusted my cause.
Sing to the LORD,
      praise the LORD,
for he has rescued the life of the poor
      from the power of the wicked!"

The word of the Lord. **Thanks be to God.**

Responsorial Psalm *(Psalm 69:8-10, 14, 17, 33-35)*

℟. **Lord, in your great love, answer me.**

For your sake I bear insult,
      and shame covers my face.
I have become an outcast to my brothers,
      a stranger to my children,
because zeal for your house consumes me,
      and the insults of those who blaspheme you
            fall upon me. ℟.
I pray to you, O LORD,
      for the time of your favor, O God!
In your great kindness answer me
      with your constant help.
Answer me, O LORD, for bounteous is your kindness;
      in your great mercy turn toward me. ℟.

"See, you lowly ones, and be glad;
    you who seek God, may your hearts revive!
For the LORD hears the poor,
    and his own who are in bonds he spurns not.
Let the heavens and the earth praise him,
    the seas and whatever moves in them!" R.

Second Reading *(Romans 5:12-15)*

Brothers and sisters: Through one man **sin entered the world**, and through sin, death, and thus death came to all men, inasmuch as all sinned—for up to the time of the law, sin was in the world, though sin is not accounted when there is no **law**. But death reigned from Adam to Moses, even over those who did not sin after the pattern of the **trespass** of Adam, who is the **type** of the one who was to come.

But the gift is not like the **transgression**. For if by the transgression of the one the many died, how much more did the grace of God and the gracious gift of the one man Jesus Christ overflow for the many.

The word of the Lord. **Thanks be to God.**

Gospel *(Matthew 10:26-33)*

A reading from the holy Gospel according to Matthew.
Glory to you, O Lord.

Jesus said to the Twelve: "Fear no one. Nothing is concealed that will not be revealed, nor secret that will not be known. What I say to you in the darkness, speak in the light; what you hear whispered, proclaim on the housetops. And do not be afraid of those who kill the body but cannot kill the soul; rather, be afraid of the one who can destroy both soul and body in Gehenna. Are not two sparrows sold for a small coin? Yet not one of them falls to the ground without your Father's knowledge. Even all the hairs of your head are counted. So do not be afraid; you are worth more than many sparrows. Everyone who acknowledges me before others I will acknowledge before my heavenly Father. But whoever denies me before others, I will deny before my heavenly Father."

The Gospel of the Lord. **Praise to you, Lord Jesus Christ.**

Key Words

A **Prophet** was a holy man or woman who spoke publicly against poverty and injustice, and criticized the people whenever they refused to listen to God's word. Many of the books of the Old Testament were written by prophets (Isaiah, Jeremiah, Amos, and Micah, for example).

Jeremiah lived about 600 years before Jesus. When Jeremiah was still a young boy, God called him to guide the people of Israel back to God. Many people ignored Jeremiah at first and sent him away. But when they faced serious problems and feared that God had stopped loving them, Jeremiah gave them hope that God would not abandon them.

In the Letter to the Romans, Saint Paul reminds us that **sin entered the world** by Adam (and Eve) in the Garden of Eden, and with sin came death. New life also came into the world by one man—Jesus Christ, the Son of God.

The **law** refers in part to the Ten Commandments that God gave to Moses at Mount Sinai. Saint Paul tells us that even though there was no "law" to break in the time between Adam and Moses, there were still sin and death in the world.

Trespass and **transgression** are other ways to talk of sin. We use the word "trespasses" to mean "sin" when we pray the Our Father.

A **type** is a model or example. Saint Paul shows us how Adam as the first human being brought sin and death into the world, and then Jesus, the son of God and first-born from the dead, brought grace and eternal life for all.

First Reading (*2 Kings 4:8-11, 14-16a*)

One day Elisha came to Shunem, where there was a woman of influence, who urged him to dine with her. Afterward, whenever he passed by, he used to stop there to dine. So she said to her husband, "I know that Elisha is a holy man of God. Since he visits us often, let us arrange a little room on the roof and furnish it for him with a bed, table, chair, and lamp, so that when he comes to us he can stay there." Sometime later Elisha arrived and stayed in the room overnight.

Later Elisha asked, "Can something be done for her?" His servant Gehazi answered, "Yes! She has no **son**, and her husband is getting on in years." Elisha said, "Call her." When the woman had been called and stood at the door, Elisha promised, "This time next year you will be fondling a baby son."

The word of the Lord. **Thanks be to God.**

Responsorial Psalm (*Psalm 89:2-3, 16-17, 18-19*)

R. **Forever I will sing the goodness of the Lord.**

The promises of the LORD I will sing forever,
   through all generations my mouth shall proclaim
      your faithfulness.
For you have said, "My kindness is established forever";
   in heaven you have confirmed your faithfulness. R.
Blessed the people who know the joyful shout;
   in the light of your countenance, O LORD, they walk.
At your name they rejoice all the day,
   and through your justice they are exalted. R.
You are the splendor of their strength,
   and by your favor our horn is exalted.
For to the LORD belongs our shield,
   and to the Holy One of Israel, our king. R.

Second Reading *(Romans 6:3-4, 8-11)*

Brothers and sisters: Are you unaware that we who were baptized into Christ Jesus were baptized into his death? We were indeed buried with him through baptism into death, so that, just as Christ was raised from the dead by the glory of the Father, we too might live in newness of life.

If, then, we have died with Christ, we believe that we shall also live with him. We know that Christ, raised from the dead, dies no more; death no longer has **power** over him. As to his death, he died to sin once and for all; as to his life, he lives for God. Consequently, you too must think of yourselves as dead to sin and living for God in Christ Jesus.

The word of the Lord. **Thanks be to God.**

Gospel *(Matthew 10:37-42)*

A reading from the holy Gospel according to Matthew.
Glory to you, O Lord.

Jesus said to his apostles: "Whoever loves father or mother more than me is not worthy of me, and whoever loves son or daughter more than me is not worthy of me; and whoever does not take up his cross and follow after me is not worthy of me. Whoever finds his life will lose it, and whoever loses his life for my sake will find it. Whoever receives you receives me, and whoever receives me receives the one who sent me. Whoever receives a prophet because he is a prophet will receive a prophet's reward, and whoever receives a righteous man because he is a righteous man will receive a righteous man's reward. And whoever gives only a cup of cold water to one of these little ones to drink because the little one is a disciple— amen, I say to you, he will surely not lose his reward.""

The Gospel of the Lord. **Praise to you, Lord Jesus Christ.**

Key Words

In the Bible, the two books of **Kings** tell the story of a time when Israel was ruled by kings. The books begin with the death of King David, nearly 1,000 years before Jesus was born, and end when the Babylonians capture Jerusalem, nearly 600 years before Jesus. The writer wants us to see how God helps his people throughout history.

Before Jesus rose from the dead, death had **power** over all people. Jesus broke death's power when he rose from the dead, bringing eternal life to all who believe.

In the ancient world, children were important for a family's future. Daughters would marry into neighboring families, and **sons** would inherit family possessions and position in the community. If the father died, the son would be responsible for caring for his mother and siblings. Elisha is blessing the wealthy woman's family for their hospitality by promising them a son.

First Reading (*Zechariah 9:9-10*)

Thus says the LORD:
Rejoice heartily, O **daughter Zion**,
　　shout for joy, O daughter Jerusalem!
See, your king shall come to you;
　　a just savior is he,
meek, and riding on an ass,
　　on a colt, the foal of an ass.
He shall banish the chariot from **Ephraim**,
　　and the horse from Jerusalem;
the warrior's bow shall be banished,
　　and he shall proclaim peace to the nations.
His dominion shall be from sea to sea,
　　and from the River to the ends of the earth.

The word of the Lord. **Thanks be to God.**

Responsorial Psalm (*145:1-2, 8-9, 10-11, 13-14*)

R. **I will praise your name forever, my king and my God.**
Or **Alleluia.**

I will extol you, O my God and King,
　　and I will bless your name forever and ever.
Every day will I bless you,
　　and I will praise your name forever and ever. R.
The LORD is gracious and merciful,
　　slow to anger and of great kindness.
The LORD is good to all
　　and compassionate toward all his works. R.
Let all your works give you thanks, O LORD,
　　and let your faithful ones bless you.
Let them discourse of the glory of your kingdom
　　and speak of your might. R.
The LORD is faithful in all his words
　　and holy in all his works.
The LORD lifts up all who are falling
　　and raises up all who are bowed down. R.

Second Reading *(Romans 8:9, 11-13)*

Brothers and sisters: You are not in the flesh; on the contrary, you are in the spirit, if only the **Spirit of God** dwells in you. Whoever does not have the Spirit of Christ does not belong to him. If the Spirit of the one who raised Jesus from the dead dwells in you, the one who raised Christ from the dead will give life to your mortal bodies also, through his Spirit that dwells in you. Consequently, brothers and sisters, we are not debtors to the flesh, to live according to the flesh. For if you live according to the flesh, you will die, but if by the Spirit you put to death the deeds of the body, you will live.

The word of the Lord. **Thanks be to God.**

Gospel *(Matthew 11:25–30)*

A reading from the holy Gospel according to Matthew.
Glory to you, O Lord.

At that time Jesus exclaimed: "I give praise to you, Father, Lord of heaven and earth, for although you have hidden these things from the wise and the learned you have revealed them to little ones. Yes, Father, such has been your gracious will. All things have been handed over to me by my Father. No one knows the Son except the Father, and no one knows the Father except the Son and anyone to whom the Son wishes to reveal him.

"Come to me, all you who labor and are **burdened**, and I will give you rest. Take my yoke upon you and learn from me, for I am meek and humble of heart; and you will find rest for yourselves. For my yoke is easy, and my burden light."

The Gospel of the Lord. **Praise to you, Lord Jesus Christ.**

Key Words

Zechariah was a prophet who lived 520 years before Christ. The temple in Jerusalem had been destroyed by Nebuchadnezzar, and Zechariah was trying to lift the spirits of the people of Israel. A good part of the book of Zechariah is dedicated to announcing the coming of the Messiah. He will come like a king, like a shepherd, or like the servant of the Lord.

Zion was the name of a hill in Jerusalem where the temple was built, but the city itself was often called Zion. **Daughter Zion** is another way of naming the entire nation, the whole People of God.

Ephraim is the name of one of Jacob's sons and one of the twelve tribes of Israel. The Bible sometimes uses this name for the whole people of Israel.

The **Spirit of God** dwells in us by speaking in our hearts and leading us to follow Jesus by our words and actions. If we listen to the Spirit and follow where it leads, we are living according to the Spirit.

The **Gospel** is the message of Jesus. It comes from an old English word *godspel* that means "good news."

Everyone is **burdened** by some things in life—times of pain or suffering. But if we live as Jesus taught us, we will also have great joy and the hard times will be easier to bear. Jesus brings us true consolation and comfort.

First Reading *(Isaiah 55:10-11)*

Thus says the LORD:
Just as from the heavens
    the rain and snow come down
and do not return there
    till they have watered the earth,
    making it fertile and fruitful,
giving seed to the one who sows
    and bread to the one who eats,
so shall my word be
    that goes forth from my mouth;
my word shall not return to me void,
    but shall do my will,
    achieving the end for which I sent it.

The word of the Lord. **Thanks be to God.**

Responsorial Psalm *(Psalm 65:10, 11, 12-13, 14)*

R. **The seed that falls on good ground will yield
a fruitful harvest.**

You have visited the land and watered it;
    greatly have you enriched it.
God's watercourses are filled;
    you have prepared the grain. R.
Thus have you prepared the land: drenching its furrows,
    breaking up its clods,
Softening it with showers,
    blessing its yield. R.
You have crowned the year with your bounty,
    and your paths overflow with a rich harvest;
The untilled meadows overflow with it,
    and rejoicing clothes the hills. R.
The fields are garmented with flocks
    and the valleys blanketed with grain.
    They shout and sing for joy. R.

Second Reading *(Romans 8:18-23)*

Brothers and sisters: I consider that the sufferings of this present time are as nothing compared with the **glory** to be revealed for us. For creation awaits with eager expectation the revelation of the children of God; for creation was made subject to **futility**, not of its own accord but because of the one who subjected it, in hope that creation itself would be set free from slavery to corruption and share in the glorious freedom of the children of God. We know that all creation is groaning in labor pains even until now; and not only that, but we ourselves, who have the firstfruits of the Spirit, we also groan within ourselves as we wait for adoption, the redemption of our bodies.

The word of the Lord. **Thanks be to God.**

Gospel *(Matthew 13:1-23)*

The shorter version ends at the asterisks.

A reading from the holy Gospel according to Matthew.
Glory to you, O Lord.

On that day, Jesus went out of the house and sat down by the sea. Such large crowds gathered around him that he got into a boat and sat down, and the whole crowd stood along the shore. And he spoke to them at length in **parables**, saying: "A **sower** went out to sow. And as he sowed, some seed fell on the path, and birds came and ate it up. Some fell on rocky ground, where it had little soil. It sprang up at once because the soil was not deep, and when the sun rose it was scorched, and it withered for lack of **roots**. Some seed fell among thorns, and the thorns grew up and choked it. But some seed fell on rich soil, and produced fruit, a hundred or sixty or thirtyfold. Whoever has ears ought to hear."

* * *

The disciples approached him and said, "Why do you speak to them in parables?" He said to them in reply, "Because knowledge of the mysteries of the kingdom of heaven has been granted to you, but to them it has not been granted. To anyone who has, more will be given and he will grow rich; from anyone who has not, even what he has will be taken away. This is why I speak to them in parables, because *they look but do not see and hear but* do not listen or understand. Isaiah's prophecy is fulfilled in them, which says:

> You shall indeed hear but not understand,
>> you shall indeed look but never see.
> Gross is the heart of this people,
>> they will hardly hear with their ears,
>> they have closed their eyes,
>> lest they see with their eyes
>> and hear with their ears
> and understand with their hearts and be converted,
>> and I heal them.

"But blessed are your eyes, because they see, and your ears, because they hear. Amen, I say to you, many prophets and righteous people longed to see what you see but did not see it, and to hear what you hear but did not hear it.

"Hear then the parable of the sower. The seed sown on the path is the one who hears the word of the kingdom without understanding it, and the evil one comes and steals away what was sown in his heart. The seed sown on rocky ground is the one who hears the word and receives it at once with joy. But he has no root and lasts only for a time. When some tribulation or persecution comes because of the word, he immediately falls away. The seed sown among thorns is the one who hears the word, but then worldly anxiety and the lure of riches choke the word and it bears no fruit. But the seed sown on rich soil is the one who hears the word and understands it, who indeed bears fruit and yields a hundred or sixty or thirtyfold."

The Gospel of the Lord. **Praise to you, Lord Jesus Christ.**

Key Words

Saul was a man who bullied and terrorized the first Christians. One day, he had a vision of the risen Jesus and the experience changed his whole life. When he was baptized he changed his name to **Paul** and became a great apostle, traveling to cities all around the Mediterranean Sea to tell people about the love of Jesus. His letters found in the Bible are the earliest books of the New Testament or Christian Scriptures.

When we speak of God's **glory**, we are talking about God's power, importance, and splendor.

When we are distracted from our friendship with God, our lives are ones of **futility** or aimlessness—they have no meaning. God wants us to direct our lives to following the Spirit.

Parables are brief stories or wise sayings that Jesus used when he was teaching. Jesus used everyday situations to help his listeners understand what he meant. The parables invite us to change our lives and turn to God.

A **sower** is a farmer who is planting seeds by hand. In this parable, the seeds represent the word of God. Sometimes it bears fruit and sometimes it does not. We must try to be fertile ground for the word of God.

A plant needs good **roots**, deep and strong, in order to survive times of stress. We also need a solid and secure faith, rooted deep in the Spirit of God, dwelling in our hearts.

JULY 23
16th Sunday in Ordinary Time

First Reading *(Wisdom 12:13, 16-19)*

There is no god besides you who have the care of all,
    that you need show you have not unjustly condemned.
For your might is the source of justice;
    your mastery over all things makes you **lenient** to all.
For you show your might when the perfection of
        your power is disbelieved;
    and in those who know you, you rebuke temerity.
But though you are master of might, you **judge** with
clemency,
    and with much lenience you govern us;
    for power, whenever you will, attends you.
And you taught your people, by these deeds,
    that those who are just must be kind;
and you gave your children good ground for hope
    that you would permit repentance for their sins.

The word of the Lord. **Thanks be to God.**

Responsorial Psalm *(Psalm 86:5-6, 9-10, 15-16)*

R̶. **Lord, you are good and forgiving.**

You, O LORD, are good and forgiving,
    abounding in kindness to all who call upon you.
Hearken, O LORD, to my prayer
    and attend to the sound of my pleading. R̶.
All the nations you have made shall come
    and worship you, O LORD,
    and glorify your name.
For you are great, and you do wondrous deeds;
    you alone are God. R̶.
You, O LORD, are a God merciful and gracious,
    slow to anger, abounding in kindness and fidelity.
Turn toward me, and have pity on me;
    give your strength to your servant. R̶.

Second Reading *(Romans 8:26-27)*

Brothers and sisters: The Spirit comes to the aid of our weakness; for we do not know how to pray as we ought, but the Spirit himself **intercedes** with inexpressible groanings. And the one who searches hearts knows what is the intention of the Spirit, because he intercedes for the holy ones according to God's will.

The word of the Lord. **Thanks be to God.**

Gospel *(Matthew 13:24-43)*

The shorter version ends at the asterisks.

A reading from the holy Gospel according to Matthew.
Glory to you, O Lord.

Jesus proposed another parable to the crowds, saying: "The kingdom of heaven may be likened to a man who sowed good seed in his field. While everyone was asleep his enemy came and sowed **weeds** all through the wheat, and then went off. When the crop grew and bore fruit, the weeds appeared as well. The slaves of the householder came to him and said, 'Master, did you not sow good seed in your field? Where have the weeds come from?' He answered, 'An enemy has done this.' His slaves said to him, 'Do you want us to go and pull them up?' He replied, 'No, if you pull up the weeds you might uproot the wheat along with them. Let them grow together until harvest; then at harvest time I will say to the harvesters, "First collect the weeds and tie them in **bundles** for burning; but gather the wheat into my barn." ' "

* * *

He proposed another parable to them. "The kingdom of heaven is like a mustard seed that a person took and sowed in a field. It is the smallest of all the seeds, yet when full-grown it is the largest of plants. It becomes a large bush, and the 'birds of the sky come and dwell in its branches.' "

He spoke to them another parable. "The kingdom of heaven is like **yeast** that a woman took and mixed with three measures of wheat flour until the whole batch was leavened."

All these things Jesus spoke to the crowds in parables. He spoke to them only in parables, to fulfill what had been said through the prophet:

> I will open my mouth in parables,
> I will announce what has lain hidden
> from the foundation of the world.

Then, dismissing the crowds, he went into the house. His disciples approached him and said, "Explain to us the parable of the weeds in the field." He said in reply, "He who sows good seed is the Son of Man, the field is the world, the good seed the children of the kingdom. The weeds are the children of the evil one, and the enemy who sows them is the devil. The harvest is the end of the age, and the harvesters are angels. Just as weeds are **collected** and **burned up** with fire, so will it be at the end of the age. The Son of Man will send his angels, and they will collect out of his kingdom all who cause others to sin and all evildoers. They will throw them into the fiery furnace, where there will be wailing and grinding of teeth. Then the righteous will shine like the sun in the kingdom of their Father. Whoever has ears ought to hear."

The Gospel of the Lord. **Praise to you, Lord Jesus Christ.**

Key Words

The book of **Wisdom** was written not long before Jesus was born. It urges us to make good decisions in life. It teaches about justice and fairness.

To be **lenient** toward someone is to decide not to punish them or to relieve them of trouble—to show them mercy.

To **judge** is to decide a question based on the evidence. For example, in court a judge may decide whether someone is innocent or guilty of a crime. God is a loving judge who shows great patience and mercy.

To **intercede** is to ask for something on behalf of another person. After Jesus rose from the dead, he sent the Holy Spirit to speak on our behalf and to dwell in our hearts.

When **weeds** grow alongside a crop, they take water and nutrition away from the good plants. A weed-free field will produce a better harvest.

At the time of harvest, both the weeds and the wheat were tied into their own **bundles**, to make them easier to handle by the fieldworkers. This separates the good plants from the bad.

A small amount of **yeast** is added to bread dough to make it rise. The bread is then light and easy to eat. A very small amount of yeast can leaven a large amount of bread—just as our kind words or good deeds can make a difference to others.

The weeds were **collected** and **burned up** by the farmer in order to prevent the weeds and their seeds from spreading. The crops will grow better if the field is weed-free.

210

First Reading *(1 Kings 3:5, 7-12)*

The LORD appeared to **Solomon** in a dream at night. God said, "Ask something of me and I will give it to you." Solomon answered: "O LORD, my God, you have made me, your servant, king to succeed my father David; but I am a mere youth, not knowing at all how to act. I serve you in the midst of the people whom you have chosen, a people so vast that it cannot be numbered or counted. Give your servant, therefore, an **understanding heart** to judge your people and to distinguish right from wrong. For who is able to govern this vast people of yours?"

The LORD was pleased that Solomon made this request. So God said to him: "Because you have asked for this—not for a long life for yourself, nor for riches, nor for the life of your enemies, but for understanding so that you may know what is right—I do as you requested. I give you a heart so wise and understanding that there has never been anyone like you up to now, and after you there will come no one to equal you."

The word of the Lord. **Thanks be to God.**

Responsorial Psalm *(Psalm 119:57, 72, 76-77, 127-128, 129-130)*

R. **Lord, I love your commands!**

I have said, O LORD, that my part
    is to keep your words.
The law of your mouth is to me more precious
    than thousands of gold and silver pieces. R.
Let your kindness comfort me
    according to your promise to your servants.
Let your compassion come to me that I may live,
    for your law is my delight. R.
For I love your commands
    more than gold, however fine.
For in all your precepts I go forward;
    every false way I hate. R.
Wonderful are your decrees;
    therefore I observe them.
The revelation of your words sheds light,
    giving understanding to the simple. R.

Second Reading *(Romans 8:28-30)*

Brothers and sisters: We know that all things work for good for those who love God, who are called according to his **purpose**. For those he foreknew he also **predestined** to be conformed to the image of his Son, so that he might be the firstborn among many brothers and sisters. And those he predestined he also called; and those he called he also **justified**; and those he justified he also glorified.

The word of the Lord. **Thanks be to God.**

Gospel *(Matthew 13:44-52)*

The shorter reading ends at the asterisks.

A reading from the holy Gospel according to Matthew.
Glory to you, O Lord.

Jesus said to his disciples: "The kingdom of heaven is like a **treasure** buried in a field, which a person finds and hides again, and out of joy goes and sells all that he has and buys that field. Again, the kingdom of heaven is like a merchant searching for fine pearls. When he finds a pearl of great price, he goes and sells all that he has and buys it.

* * *

Again, the kingdom of heaven is like a net thrown into the sea, which collects fish of every kind. When it is full they haul it ashore and sit down to put what is good into buckets. What is bad they throw away. Thus it will be at the end of the age. The angels will go out and separate the wicked from the righteous and throw them into the fiery furnace, where there will be wailing and grinding of teeth.

"Do you understand all these things?" They answered, "Yes." And he replied, "Then every scribe who has been instructed in the kingdom of heaven is like the head of a household who brings from his storeroom both the new and the old."

The Gospel of the Lord. **Praise to you, Lord Jesus Christ.**

Solomon was the king of Israel after his father, David. He lived 1,000 years before Christ. Solomon was a wise and prudent king.

A person with an **understanding heart** relies not only on what the brain knows, but also on the wisdom of the heart. Solomon knew God as the Creator of all and made his decisions based on this deep knowledge.

God's **purpose** from the beginning has been the salvation of all creation. God wants all humankind to live in friendship with him.

God knows us before we are born, and we are **predestined** or meant to be God's children. We should live like Jesus did, loving the Father and taking care of others, especially those who are weaker or in need. This is the destiny God has for us.

When we hurt others, we break our friendship with God. But Jesus came to restore our friendship with God, and we are **justified** or brought back to friendship with God by our faith in Jesus.

By comparing the kingdom of heaven to **treasure**, Jesus is saying that life with God is more valuable than anything we can find or buy on earth. It is priceless.

AUGUST 6
The Transfiguration of the Lord

First Reading *(Daniel 7:9-10, 13-14)*

As I watched:
 Thrones were set up
  and the **Ancient One** took his throne.
 His clothing was bright as snow,
  and the hair on his head as white as wool;
 His throne was flames of fire,
  with wheels of burning fire.
 A surging stream of fire
  flowed out from where he sat;
 Thousands upon thousands were ministering to him,
  and myriads upon myriads attended him.
 The court was convened and the books were opened.
As the visions during the night continued, I saw:
 One like a Son of man coming,
  on the clouds of heaven;
 When he reached the Ancient One
  and was presented before him,
 The one like a Son of man received **dominion**, glory, and kingship;
  all peoples, nations, and languages serve him.
 His dominion is an everlasting dominion
  that shall not be taken away,
  his kingship shall not be destroyed.

The word of the Lord. **Thanks be to God.**

Responsorial Psalm *(Psalm 97:1-2, 5-6, 9)*

R. **The Lord is king, the Most High over all the earth.**

 The LORD is king; let the earth rejoice;
  let the many islands be glad.
 Clouds and darkness are round about him,
  justice and judgment are the foundation
   of his throne. R.
 The mountains melt like wax before the LORD,
  before the LORD of all the earth.
 The heavens proclaim his justice,
  and all peoples see his glory. R.
 Because you, O LORD, are the Most High over all the earth,
  exalted far above all gods. R.

Second Reading *(2 Peter 1:16-19)*

Beloved: We did not follow cleverly devised myths when we made known to you the power and coming of our Lord Jesus Christ, but we had been **eyewitnesses** of his majesty. For he received honor and glory from God the Father when that unique declaration came to him from the majestic glory, "This is my Son, my beloved, with whom I am well pleased." We ourselves heard this voice come from heaven while we were with him on the holy mountain. Moreover, we possess the prophetic message that is altogether reliable. You will do well to be attentive to it, as to a lamp shining in a dark place, until day dawns and the morning star rises in your hearts.

The word of the Lord. **Thanks be to God.**

Gospel *(Matthew 17:1-9)*

A reading from the holy Gospel according to Matthew.
Glory to you, O Lord.

Jesus took Peter, James, and his brother, John, and led them up a high mountain by themselves. And he was **transfigured** before them; his face shone like the sun and his clothes became white as light. And behold, Moses and **Elijah** appeared to them, conversing with him. Then Peter said to Jesus in reply, "Lord, it is good that we are here. If you wish, I will make three tents here, one for you, one for Moses, and one for Elijah." While he was still speaking, behold, a bright cloud cast a shadow over them, then from the cloud came a voice that said, "This is my beloved Son, with whom I am well pleased; listen to him." When the disciples heard this, they fell prostrate and were very much afraid. But Jesus came and touched them, saying, "Rise, and do not be afraid." And when the disciples raised their eyes, they saw no one else but Jesus alone.

As they were coming down from the mountain, Jesus charged them, "Do not tell the vision to anyone until the Son of Man has been raised from the dead."

The Gospel of the Lord. **Praise to you, Lord Jesus Christ.**

Key Words

The **book of Daniel** gave the Hebrew people comfort and hope in hard times. It was written about 160 years before Jesus was born, and is the first book of the Bible to talk about the resurrection of the dead.

Daniel calls God the **Ancient One** as a way to show how God is eternal—his kingdom will have no end.

Dominion is a word meaning the authority to govern. To the Hebrew people, God's dominion extended to all peoples, all creation, heaven and hell. God is ruler over all.

Saint Peter was fortunate in that he actually knew Jesus— he and the other disciples were **eyewitnesses** to Jesus' teachings, his miracles, and his passion and resurrection. While we cannot say the same, we do have their eyewitness accounts to guide us and strengthen us in our faith.

When Jesus was **transfigured**, he was changed and looked different somehow. His friends saw who Jesus really is: the Son of God.

The prophet **Elijah** lived about 900 years before Jesus. He taught the people about God. He is one of the great prophets in the Old Testament or Hebrew Scriptures.

First Reading *(1 Kings 19:9a, 11-13a)*

At the mountain of God, **Horeb**, Elijah came to a cave where he took shelter. Then the LORD said to him, "Go outside and stand on the mountain before the LORD; the LORD will be passing by." A strong and heavy wind was rending the mountains and crushing rocks before the LORD—but the LORD was not in the wind. After the wind there was an earthquake—but the LORD was not in the earthquake. After the earthquake there was fire—but the LORD was not in the fire. After the fire there was a tiny whispering sound. When he heard this, Elijah hid his face in his cloak and went and stood at the entrance of the cave.

The word of the Lord. **Thanks be to God.**

Responsorial Psalm *(Psalm 85:9, 10, 11-12, 13-14)*

℟. **Lord, let us see your kindness, and grant us your salvation.**

I will hear what God proclaims;
    the LORD—for he proclaims peace.
Near indeed is his salvation to those who fear him,
    glory dwelling in our land. ℟.
Kindness and truth shall meet;
    justice and peace shall kiss.
Truth shall spring out of the earth,
    and justice shall look down from heaven. ℟.
The LORD himself will give his benefits;
    our land shall yield its increase.
Justice shall walk before him,
    and prepare the way of his steps. ℟.

Second Reading *(Romans 9:1-5)*

Brothers and sisters: I speak the truth in Christ, I do not lie; my conscience joins with the Holy Spirit in bearing me witness that I have great sorrow and constant anguish in my heart. For I could wish that I myself were accursed and cut off from Christ for the sake of my own people, my kindred according to the flesh. They are Israelites; theirs the adoption, the glory, the covenants, the giving of the law, the worship, and the promises; theirs the **patriarchs**, and from them, according to the flesh, is the Christ, who is over all, God blessed forever. **Amen**.

The word of the Lord. **Thanks be to God.**

Gospel *(Matthew 14:22-33)*

A reading from the holy Gospel according to Matthew.
Glory to you, O Lord.

After he had fed the people, Jesus made the disciples get into a boat and precede him to the other side, while he dismissed the crowds. After doing so, he went up on the mountain by himself to pray. When it was evening he was there alone. Meanwhile the boat, already a few miles offshore, was being tossed about by the waves, for the wind was against it. During the fourth watch of the night, he came toward them walking on the sea. When the disciples saw him walking on the sea they were terrified. "It is a ghost, " they said, and they cried out in fear. At once Jesus spoke to them, "Take courage, it is I; do not be afraid." Peter said to him in reply, "Lord, if it is you, command me to come to you on the water." He said, "Come." Peter got out of the boat and began to walk on the water toward Jesus. But when he saw how strong the wind was he became frightened; and, beginning to sink, he cried out, "Lord, save me!" Immediately Jesus stretched out his hand and caught Peter, and said to him, "O you of little faith, why did you doubt?" After they got into the boat, the wind died down. Those who were in the boat **did him homage**, saying, "Truly, you are the Son of God."

The Gospel of the Lord. **Praise to you, Lord Jesus Christ.**

Key Words

Mount **Horeb** (or Mount Sinai, as it is also called) is a place where God often visited his people. God spoke to Moses there and gave him the Ten Commandments.

The **patriarchs** were the ancestors of the people of Israel. Abraham, Isaac, and Jacob were all known as patriarchs. God promised them that this people would become a great nation.

Amen is a Hebrew word that means "so be it" or "I know this is true." By saying "Amen" after hearing or saying a prayer, we are agreeing with what it says. We say "Amen" many times during Mass, especially after the Eucharistic Prayer when we sing the Great Amen, showing that we join with the priest in this great hymn of praise.

After Jesus walked on water, the apostles **did him homage** because they recognized that he was more than a man. Jesus is true God and true man. Worship is a gesture that recognizes the greatness of the one being worshipped.

AUGUST 20

20th Sunday in Ordinary Time

First Reading *(Isaiah 56:1, 6-7)*

Thus says the LORD:
>Observe what is right, **do what is just**;
>>for my salvation is about to come,
>>my justice, about to be revealed.

>The foreigners who join themselves to the LORD,
>>ministering to him,
>loving the name of the LORD,
>>and becoming his servants—
>all who **keep the sabbath** free from profanation
>>and hold to my covenant,
>them I will bring to my holy mountain
>>and make joyful in my house of prayer;
>their **burnt offerings** and sacrifices
>>will be acceptable on my altar,
>for my house shall be called
>>a house of prayer for all peoples.

The word of the Lord. **Thanks be to God.**

Responsorial Psalm *(Psalm 67:2-3, 5, 6, 8)*

R. **O God, let all the nations praise you!**

>May God have pity on us and bless us;
>>may he let his face shine upon us.
>So may your way be known upon earth;
>>among all nations, your salvation. R.
>May the nations be glad and exult
>>because you rule the peoples in equity;
>>the nations on the earth you guide. R.
>May the peoples praise you, O God;
>>may all the peoples praise you!
>May God bless us,
>>and may all the ends of the earth fear him! R.

Second Reading *(Romans 11:13-15, 29-32)*

Brothers and sisters: I am speaking to you Gentiles. Inasmuch as I am the **apostle to the Gentiles**, I glory in my ministry in order to make my race jealous and thus save some of them. For if their rejection is the reconciliation of the world, what will their acceptance be but life from the dead?

For the gifts and the call of God are irrevocable. Just as you once disobeyed God but have now received mercy because of their disobedience, so they have now disobeyed in order that, by virtue of the mercy shown to you, they too may now receive mercy. For God delivered all to disobedience, that he might have mercy upon all.

The word of the Lord. **Thanks be to God.**

Gospel *(Matthew 15:21-28)*

A reading from the holy Gospel according to Matthew.
Glory to you, O Lord.

At that time, Jesus withdrew to the region of Tyre and Sidon. And behold, a **Canaanite** woman of that district came and called out, "Have pity on me, Lord, Son of David! My daughter is tormented by a demon." But Jesus did not say a word in answer to her. Jesus' disciples came and asked him, "Send her away, for she keeps calling out after us." He said in reply, "I was sent only to the lost sheep of the **house of Israel**." But the woman came and did Jesus homage, saying, "Lord, help me." He said in reply, "It is not right to take the food of the children and throw it to the dogs." She said, "Please, Lord, for even the dogs eat the scraps that fall from the table of their masters." Then Jesus said to her in reply, "O woman, **great is your faith**! Let it be done for you as you wish." And the woman's daughter was healed from that hour.

The Gospel of the Lord. **Praise to you, Lord Jesus Christ.**

Our faith in God requires us to **do what is just**—to take care of the rights of others. Working for the dignity and freedom of others is one way of obeying God's commandments.

The Sabbath is the day of the week when human beings rest as God did on the seventh day of creation. It is a chance for us to spend time praising God and enjoying creation. One of the Ten Commandments instructs us to **keep the Sabbath** holy.

Burnt offerings are a type of sacrifice to God where a dead animal (such as a lamb or calf) is put on a fire. Another type of offering is a libation or drink-offering that is poured out.

Saint Paul calls himself an **apostle to the Gentiles**, meaning a messenger to people who were not Jewish.

He wants all people, Jews and Gentiles, to be saved from death by faith in Jesus.

Canaanites were people from Canaan. After forty years in the desert, Moses brought the people to the land of Canaan, the promised land. In the time of Jesus, people from Canaan were considered foreigners.

House of Israel is one of the many names for the Israelites. Other names include House of David and House of Judah.

When Jesus says, "**great is your faith**," he is pointing to the confidence the Canaanite woman has. She asks Jesus to heal her daughter's illness and her own pain, believing that he will help them, even though they are strangers in Jewish society.

First Reading *(Isaiah 22:19-23)*

Thus says the LORD to **Shebna**, master of the palace:
"I will thrust you from your office
    and pull you down from your station.
On that day I will summon my servant
    Eliakim, son of Hilkiah;
I will clothe him with your robe,
    and gird him with your sash,
    and give over to him your authority.
He shall be a father to the inhabitants of Jerusalem,
    and to the **house of Judah**.
I will place the key of the House of David on Eliakim's shoulder;
    when he opens, no one shall shut;
    when he shuts, no one shall open.
I will fix him like a peg in a sure spot,
    to be a place of honor for his family."

The word of the Lord. **Thanks be to God.**

Responsorial Psalm *(Psalm 138:1-2, 2-3, 6, 8)*

R. **Lord, your love is eternal; do not forsake the work of your hands.**

I will give thanks to you, O LORD, with all my heart,
    for you have heard the words of my mouth;
in the presence of the angels I will sing your praise;
    I will worship at your holy temple. R.
I will give thanks to your name,
    because of your kindness and your truth:
When I called, you answered me;
    you built up strength within me. R.
The LORD is exalted, yet the lowly he sees,
    and the proud he knows from afar.
Your kindness, O LORD, endures forever;
    forsake not the work of your hands. R.

Second Reading *(Romans 11:33-36)*

Oh, the depth of the riches and wisdom and knowledge of God! How inscrutable are his judgments and how unsearchable his ways!

> *For who has known the mind of the Lord*
> *or who has been his counselor?*
> *Or who has given the Lord anything*
> *that he may be repaid?*

For from him and through him and for him are all things. To him be glory forever. Amen.

The word of the Lord. **Thanks be to God.**

Gospel *(Matthew 16:13-20)*

A reading from the holy Gospel according to Matthew.
Glory to you, O Lord.

Jesus went into the region of Caesarea Philippi and he asked his disciples, "Who do people say that the **Son of Man** is?" They replied, "Some say John the Baptist, others Elijah, still others Jeremiah or one of the prophets." He said to them, "But who do you say that I am?" Simon Peter said in reply, "You are the **Christ**, the Son of the living God." Jesus said to him in reply, "Blessed are you, Simon son of Jonah. For flesh and blood has not revealed this to you, but my heavenly Father. And so I say to you, you are **Peter**, and upon this **rock** I will build my church, and the gates of the netherworld shall not prevail against it. I will give you the **keys** to the kingdom of heaven. Whatever you **bind** on earth shall be bound in heaven; and whatever you loose on earth shall be loosed in heaven." Then he strictly ordered his disciples to tell no one that he was the Christ.

The Gospel of the Lord. **Praise to you, Lord Jesus Christ.**

Key Words

Shebna's error was to construct a luxurious tomb at a time when many people were in great need. He should have used his wealth in a just way to take care of the needs of others, rather than to glorify himself.

House of Judah is one of the many names for the Israelites. Other names include House of David and House of Israel.

When Jesus began to preach, he called himself the **Son of Man**. This is another way of telling us that he was sent by God.

The Greek word for "anointed" is **Christ**. The chosen person was anointed or blessed with holy oil and given a special mission. The Aramaic word meaning "anointed" is "Messiah" (Jesus and his disciples spoke Aramaic).

When Simon shows both his understanding and faith in Jesus as the Messiah, Jesus gives him a new name—**Peter** (from the Greek word *petra* for *rock* or stone). In many other languages, the name Peter is also related to rock or stone (such as *Pierre* in French). Jesus is saying that Peter's faith will be the foundation for the Church's future.

Keys are a symbol of power. Whoever has the keys can enter and leave at will; they can also allow or deny entry to others. Jesus uses this symbol to show that Saint Peter is the person with this power in the early Church.

When Jesus promises Peter, "Whatever you **bind** on earth will be bound in heaven," he is letting Peter know that Jesus will be with him always, guiding his thoughts and actions through the presence of the Holy Spirit.

SEPTEMBER 3

22nd Sunday in Ordinary Time

First Reading *(Jeremiah 20:7-9)*

You duped me, O LORD, and I let myself be duped;
>   you were too strong for me, and you triumphed.
All the day I am an object of laughter;
>   everyone mocks me.
Whenever I speak, I must cry out,
>   violence and outrage is my message;
the word of the LORD has brought me
>   derision and reproach all the day.
I say to myself, I will not mention him,
>   I will speak in his name no more.
But then it becomes like **fire** burning in my heart,
>   imprisoned in my bones;
I grow weary holding it in, I cannot endure it.

The word of the Lord. **Thanks be to God.**

Responsorial Psalm *(Psalm 63:2, 3-4, 5-6, 8-9)*

R. **My soul is thirsting for you, O Lord my God.**

O God, you are my God whom I seek;
>   for you my flesh pines and my soul thirsts
>   like the earth, parched, lifeless and without water. R.
Thus have I gazed toward you in the sanctuary
>   to see your power and your glory,
for your kindness is a greater good than life;
>   my lips shall glorify you. R.
Thus will I bless you while I live;
>   lifting up my hands, I will call upon your name.
As with the riches of a banquet shall my soul be satisfied,
>   and with exultant lips my mouth shall praise you. R.
You are my help,
>   and in the shadow of your wings I shout for joy.
My soul clings fast to you;
>   your right hand upholds me. R.

Second Reading *(Romans 12:1-2)*

I urge you, brothers and sisters, by the mercies of God, to offer your bodies as a living sacrifice, holy and pleasing to God, your **spiritual worship**. Do not conform yourselves to this age but be transformed by the renewal of your mind, that you may discern what is the will of God, what is good and pleasing and perfect.

The word of the Lord. **Thanks be to God.**

Gospel *(Matthew 16:21-27)*

A reading from the holy Gospel according to Matthew.
Glory to you, O Lord.

Jesus began to show his disciples that he must go to Jerusalem and suffer greatly from the elders, the chief priests, and the scribes, and be killed and on the third day be raised. Then Peter took Jesus aside and began to rebuke him, "God forbid, Lord! No such thing shall ever happen to you." He turned and said to Peter, "Get behind me, **Satan**! You are an obstacle to me. You are thinking not as God does, but as human beings do."
Then Jesus said to his disciples, "Whoever wishes to come after me must deny himself, take up his **cross**, and follow me. For whoever wishes to save his life will lose it, but whoever loses his life for my sake will find it. What profit would there be for one to gain the whole world and forfeit his life? Or what can one give in exchange for his life? For the Son of Man will come with his angels in his Father's glory, and then he will repay all according to his conduct."

The Gospel of the Lord. **Praise to you, Lord Jesus Christ.**

Key Words

Jeremiah lived about 600 years before Jesus. When Jeremiah was still a young boy, God called him to guide the people of Israel back to God. Many people ignored Jeremiah at first and sent him away. But when they faced serious problems and feared that God had stopped loving them, Jeremiah gave them hope that God would not abandon them.

Jeremiah found being a prophet very hard work and he wanted to give it up. But he found he couldn't because the voice of God within him was like an intense **fire** that he could not ignore.

Saint Paul reminds us that God does not want elaborate or expensive sacrifices when we worship. God wants us to offer ourselves and our lives. Paul calls this our **spiritual worship**.

Satan is one of the names given to the enemy of God and our strongest enemy. Satan works against God and tries to lead people away from God's love. Other names for Satan are the Evil One, Lucifer, or the Devil.

To take up our **cross** means to accept all that comes with being human, the good and the bad alike, because we are called to follow the path taken by Jesus.

First Reading *(Ezekiel 33:7-9)*

Thus says the LORD: You, son of man, I have appointed **watchman** for the house of Israel; when you hear me say anything, you shall warn them for me. If I tell the wicked, "O wicked one, you shall surely die," and you do not speak out to dissuade the wicked from his way, the wicked shall die for his guilt, but I will hold you responsible for his death. But if you warn the wicked, trying to turn him from his way, and he refuses to turn from his way, he shall die for his guilt, but you shall save yourself.

The word of the Lord. **Thanks be to God.**

Responsorial Psalm *(Psalm 95:1-2, 6-7, 8-9)*

R. **If today you hear his voice, harden not your hearts.**

Come, let us sing joyfully to the LORD;
   let us acclaim the rock of our salvation.
Let us come into his presence with thanksgiving;
   let us joyfully sing psalms to him. R.
Come, let us bow down in worship;
   let us kneel before the LORD who made us.
For he is our God,
      and we are the people he shepherds,
         the flock he guides. R.
Oh, that today you would hear his voice:
   "Harden not your hearts as at Meribah,
      as in the day of Massah in the desert,
where your fathers tempted me;
      they tested me though they had seen my works." R.

Second Reading *(Romans 13:8-10)*

Brothers and sisters: Owe nothing to anyone, except to **love one another**; for the one who loves another has fulfilled the law. The commandments, "You shall not commit adultery; you shall not kill; you shall not steal; you shall not covet," and whatever other commandment there may be, are summed up in this saying, namely, "You shall love your neighbor as yourself." Love does no evil to the neighbor; hence, love is the fulfillment of the law.

The word of the Lord. **Thanks be to God.**

Gospel *(Matthew 18:15-20)*

A reading from the holy Gospel according to Matthew.
Glory to you, O Lord.

Jesus said to his disciples: "If your brother sins against you, **go and tell** him his fault between you and him alone. If he listens to you, you have won over your brother. If he does not listen, take one or two others along with you, so that 'every fact may be established on the testimony of two or three witnesses.' If he refuses to listen to them, tell the church. If he refuses to listen even to the church, then treat him as you would a **Gentile** or a **tax collector**. Amen, I say to you, whatever you bind on earth shall be bound in heaven, and whatever you loose on earth shall be loosed in heaven. Again, amen, I say to you, if two of you agree on earth about anything for which they are to pray, it shall be granted to them by my heavenly Father. For **where two or three are gathered together in my name**, there am I in the midst of them."

The Gospel of the Lord. **Praise to you, Lord Jesus Christ.**

Ezekiel was the **watchman** or look-out for Israel because it was his mission to teach the people how to live as God wants and to warn them away from error and danger.

Love one another—these words sum up what every Christian must do. All the commandments and all that Jesus said and did have their foundation in this simple phrase.

Jesus tells us to **go and tell** our friends anything we see them doing that we feel is wrong. But Jesus also tells us to do this with love in our hearts, with respect for the other person.

Gentiles are people who are not Jewish. At the time of Jesus, Gentiles could not participate fully in Jewish society because they were excluded from temple life.

The Jews didn't like **tax collectors** because they worked for the Romans who were enemies of Israel. Also, many tax collectors cheated people and took more money than they needed for taxes.

Jesus shows us that God listens to our prayers. It is especially important to pray with others—"**where two or three are gathered together in my name**"—with all people who believe in God.

SEPTEMBER 17

24th Sunday in Ordinary Time

First Reading *(Sirach 27:30–28:7)*

Wrath and anger are **hateful things**,
　　yet the sinner hugs them tight.
The vengeful will suffer the LORD's vengeance,
　　for he remembers their sins in detail.
Forgive your neighbor's injustice;
　　then when you pray, your own sins will be forgiven.
Could anyone nourish anger against another
　　and expect healing from the LORD?
Could anyone refuse mercy to another like himself,
　　can he seek pardon for his own sins?
If one who is but flesh cherishes wrath,
　　who will forgive his sins?
Remember your last days, set enmity aside;
　　remember death and decay, and cease from sin!
Think of the commandments, hate not your neighbor;
　　remember the Most High's covenant, and overlook faults.

The word of the Lord. **Thanks be to God.**

Responsorial Psalm *(Psalm 103:1-2, 3-4, 9-10, 11-12)*

℞. **The Lord is kind and merciful, slow to anger,
and rich in compassion.**

Bless the LORD, O my soul;
　　and all my being, bless his holy name.
Bless the LORD, O my soul,
　　and forget not all his benefits. ℞.
He pardons all your **iniquities**,
　　heals all your ills.
redeems your life from destruction,
　　he crowns you with kindness and compassion. ℞.
He will not always chide,
　　nor does he keep his wrath forever.
Not according to our sins does he deal with us,
　　nor does he requite us according to our crimes. ℞.
For as the heavens are high above the earth,
　　so surpassing is his kindness toward those
　　　　who fear him.
As far as the east is from the west,
　　so far has he put our **transgressions** from us. ℞.

Second Reading *(Romans 14:7-9)*

Brothers and sisters: None of us lives for oneself, and no one dies for oneself. For if we live, we live for the Lord, and if we die, we die for the Lord; so then, whether we live or die, we are the Lord's. For this is why Christ died and came to life, that he might be Lord of both the dead and the living.

The word of the Lord. **Thanks be to God.**

Gospel *(Matthew 18:21-35)*

A reading from the holy Gospel according to Matthew.
Glory to you, O Lord.

Peter approached Jesus and asked him, "Lord, if my brother sins against me, how often must I forgive? As many as **seven** times?" Jesus answered, "I say to you, not seven times but **seventy-seven times**. That is why the kingdom of heaven may be likened to a king who decided to settle accounts with his servants. When he began the accounting, a debtor was brought before him who owed him a huge amount. Since he had no way of paying it back, his master ordered him to be sold, along with his wife, his children, and all his property, in payment of the debt. At that, the servant fell down, did him homage, and said, 'Be patient with me, and I will pay you back in full.' Moved with compassion the master of that servant let him go and forgave him the loan. When that servant had left, he found one of his fellow servants who owed him a much smaller amount. He seized one of his fellow servants and started to choke him, demanding, 'Pay back what you owe.' Falling to his knees, his fellow servant begged him, 'Be patient with me, and I will pay you back.' But he refused. Instead, he had the fellow servant put in prison until he paid back the debt. Now when his fellow servants saw what had happened, they were deeply disturbed, and went to their master and reported the whole affair. His master summoned him and said to him, 'You wicked servant! I forgave you your entire debt because you begged me to. Should you not have had pity on your fellow servant, as I had pity on you?' Then in anger his master handed him over to the torturers until he should pay back the whole debt. So will my heavenly Father do to you, unless each of you forgives your brother from your heart."

The Gospel of the Lord. **Praise to you, Lord Jesus Christ.**

Key Words

In the first reading, Sirach is reminding us that when we hold onto **hateful things,** like our anger, and wish evil on another person, we are offending God in the strongest possible way.

This verse in the reading, telling us to **forgive** our neighbor, sounds just like part of the Our Father: *Forgive us our trespasses, as we forgive those who trespass against us.* From the very beginning, God has called his people to be a forgiving people.

Iniquities and **transgressions** are other words for sins or trespasses—things we do to other people that are wrong, unjust, or unkind.

The number **seven** indicates something complete, like seven days in a week—so Saint Peter is suggesting that forgiving seven times would be enough. But Jesus replies with **seventy-seven**—a super-seven—to show that we must never stop forgiving others.

First Reading *(Isaiah 55:6-9)*

Seek the LORD while he may be found,
    call him while he is near.
Let the scoundrel **forsake** his way,
    and the wicked his thoughts;
let him turn to the LORD for mercy;
    to our God, who is generous in forgiving.
For my **thoughts** are not your thoughts,
    nor are your ways my ways, says the LORD.
As high as the heavens are above the earth,
    so high are my ways above your ways
    and my thoughts above your thoughts.

The word of the Lord. **Thanks be to God.**

Responsorial Psalm *(Psalm 145:2-3, 8-9, 17-18)*

R. **The Lord is near to all who call upon him.**

Every day will I bless you,
    and I will praise your name forever and ever.
Great is the LORD and highly to be praised;
    his greatness is unsearchable. R.
The LORD is gracious and merciful,
    slow to anger and of great kindness.
The LORD is good to all
    and compassionate toward all his works. R.
The LORD is just in all his ways
    and holy in all his works.
The LORD is near to all who call upon him,
    to all who call upon him in truth. R.

Second Reading *(Philippians 1:20c-24, 27a)*

Brothers and sisters: Christ will be **magnified** in my body,
whether by life or by death. For to me life is Christ, and death
is gain. If I go on living in the flesh, that means fruitful labor
for me. And I do not know which I shall choose. I am caught
between the two. I long to depart this life and be with Christ, for

that is far better. Yet that I remain in the flesh is more necessary for your benefit.

Only, conduct yourselves in a way worthy of the gospel of Christ.

The word of the Lord. **Thanks be to God.**

Gospel *(Matthew 20:1-16a)*

A reading from the holy Gospel according to Matthew.
Glory to you, O Lord.

Jesus told his disciples this parable: "The **kingdom of heaven** is like a landowner who went out at dawn to hire laborers for his **vineyard**. After agreeing with them for the usual daily wage, he sent them into his vineyard. Going out about nine o'clock, the landowner saw others standing idle in the marketplace, and he said to them, 'You too go into my vineyard, and I will give you what is just.' So they went off. And he went out again around noon, and around three o'clock, and did likewise. Going out about five o'clock, the landowner found others standing around, and said to them, 'Why do you stand here idle all day?' They answered, 'Because no one has hired us.' He said to them, 'You too go into my vineyard.' When it was evening the owner of the vineyard said to his foreman, 'Summon the laborers and give them their pay, beginning with the last and ending with the first.' When those who had started about five o'clock came, each received the usual daily wage. So when the first came, they thought that they would receive more, but each of them also got the usual wage. And on receiving it they grumbled against the landowner, saying, 'These last ones worked only one hour, and you have made them equal to us, who bore the day's burden and the heat.' He said to one of them in reply, 'My friend, I am not cheating you. Did you not agree with me for the usual daily wage? Take what is yours and go. What if I wish to give this last one the same as you? Or am I not free to do as I wish with my own money? Are you envious because I am generous?' Thus, the last will be first, and the first will be last."

The Gospel of the Lord. **Praise to you, Lord Jesus Christ.**

Key Words

To **forsake** means to abandon or give up something. Isaiah was telling the people of Israel that they had fallen away from God and needed to journey back to the Lord their God, giving up their wicked ways.

God's **thoughts** are wise and loving, full of compassion and mercy. We can trust in God, even though we cannot understand the greatness of God.

When he was in prison Saint Paul wrote to the **Philippians**, a community of Christians living in Philippi in Greece. He thanked them for their help and encouraged them to strengthen their faith in Jesus.

Saint Paul reminds us that when we hear the word of God and act on it, Jesus is **magnified** or praised through our actions.

In the **kingdom of heaven**, all people will be brought together in Jesus. We will all live like brothers and sisters, sharing in God's abundant love and mercy.

A **vineyard** is a farm where grapevines are grown. At the time of Jesus, there were many vineyards in Israel. Grapes are an important crop because wine is made from the grapes.

OCTOBER 1
26th Sunday in Ordinary Time

First Reading *(Ezekiel 18:25-28)*

Thus says the LORD: You say, "The LORD's way is not fair!" Hear now, house of Israel: Is it my way that is unfair, or rather, are not your ways unfair? When someone **virtuous** turns away from virtue to commit **iniquity**, and dies, it is because of the iniquity he committed that he must die. But if he turns from the wickedness he has committed, he does what is right and just, he shall preserve his life; since he has turned away from all the sins that he has committed, he shall surely live, he shall not die.

The word of the Lord. **Thanks be to God.**

Responsorial Psalm *(Psalm 25:4-5, 6-7, 8-9)*

R. **Remember your mercies, O Lord.**

Your ways, O LORD, make known to me;
    teach me your paths,
guide me in your truth and teach me,
    for you are God my savior. R.
Remember that your compassion, O LORD,
    and your love are from of old.
The sins of my youth and my frailties remember not;
    in your kindness remember me,
    because of your goodness, O LORD. R.
Good and upright is the LORD;
    thus he shows sinners the way.
He guides the humble to justice,
    and he teaches the humble his way R.

Second Reading *(Philippians 2:1-11)*

The shorter version ends at the asterisks.

Brothers and sisters: If there is any encouragement in Christ, any solace in love, any participation in the Spirit, any compassion and mercy, complete my joy by being of the same mind, with the same love, united in heart, thinking one thing. Do nothing out of selfishness or out of vainglory; rather, **humbly** regard others as more important than yourselves, each looking out not for his own interests, but also for those of others.

   Have in you the same attitude that is also in Christ Jesus.

Who, though he was in the form of God,
    did not regard equality with God
    something to be grasped.
Rather, he emptied himself,
    taking the form of a slave,
    coming in human likeness;
    and found human in appearance,
    he humbled himself,
    becoming obedient to the point of death,
    even death on a cross.
Because of this, God greatly exalted him
    and bestowed on him the name
    which is above every name,
    that at the name of Jesus
    every knee should bend,
    of those in heaven and on earth and under the earth,
    and every tongue confess that
    Jesus Christ is Lord,
    to the glory of God the Father.

The word of the Lord. **Thanks be to God.**

Gospel *(Matthew 21:28-32)*

A reading from the holy Gospel according to Matthew.
Glory to you, O Lord.

Jesus said to the chief priests and elders of the people: "What is your opinion? A man had two sons. He came to the first and said, 'Son, go out and work in the vineyard today.' He said in reply, 'I will not,' but afterwards **changed his mind** and went. The man came to the other son and gave the same order. He said in reply, 'Yes, sir,' but did not go. Which of the two did his father's will?" They answered, "The first." Jesus said to them, "Amen, I say to you, tax collectors and prostitutes are entering the kingdom of God before you. When John came to you in the way of righteousness, you did not believe him; but tax collectors and prostitutes did. Yet even when you saw that, you did not later change your minds and believe him."

The Gospel of the Lord. **Praise to you, Lord Jesus Christ.**

Ezekiel was one of the most important prophets in Israel. He lived during a time when many of the people of Jerusalem were taken prisoner and forced to live in exile, in Babylon. The king and Ezekiel were taken away, too. Ezekiel helped the people follow God's ways even though they were far from home.

In the Old Testament, to be **virtuous** means to follow the laws Moses gave to the people of Israel. This is the way to life in God; a life of sin is the way to death.

Iniquity is another word for sin. It is related to the word 'unequal' and means something that is very unjust or unfair—something that is wicked.

To be **humble** means to know we are children of God without feeling too important. We accept all the qualities God gave us—the ones we think are not so good as well as our talents or the things we do well.

When the son in the parable **changed his mind**, he regretted his earlier decision. He wanted to be an obedient child and show by his actions that he loved his father. In our lives, our actions should show that we are followers of Jesus.

First Reading *(Isaiah 5:1-7)*

Let me now sing of my friend,
    my friend's song concerning his vineyard.
My friend had a vineyard
    on a fertile hillside;
he spaded it, cleared it of stones,
    and planted the choicest vines;
within it he built a watchtower,
    and hewed out a wine press.
Then he looked for the crop of grapes,
    but what it yielded was wild grapes.

Now, inhabitants of Jerusalem and people of Judah,
    judge between me and my vineyard:
What more was there to do for my vineyard
    that I had not done?
Why, when I looked for the crop of grapes,
    did it bring forth wild grapes?
Now, I will let you know
    what I mean to do with my vineyard:
take away its hedge, give it to grazing,
    break through its wall, let it be trampled!
Yes, I will make it a **ruin**:
    it shall not be pruned or hoed,
    but overgrown with thorns and **briers**;
I will command the clouds
    not to send rain upon it.
The vineyard of the LORD of hosts is the house of Israel,
    and the people of Judah are his cherished plant;
he looked for judgment, but see, **bloodshed**!
    for justice, but hark, the outcry!

The word of the Lord. **Thanks be to God.**

Responsorial Psalm *(Psalm 80:9, 12, 13-14, 15-16, 19-20)*

℞. **The vineyard of the Lord is the house of Israel.**

A vine from Egypt you transplanted;
    you drove away the nations and planted it.
It put forth its foliage to the Sea,
    its shoots as far as the River. ℞.
Why have you broken down its walls,
    so that every passer-by plucks its fruit,
the boar from the forest lays it waste,
    and the beasts of the field feed upon it? ℞.
Once again, O LORD of hosts,
    look down from heaven, and see;
take care of this vine,
    and protect what your right hand has planted,
    the son of man whom you yourself made strong. ℞.
Then we will no more withdraw from you;
    give us new life, and we will call upon your name.
O LORD, God of hosts, restore us;
    if your face shine upon us, then we shall be saved. ℞.

Second Reading *(Philippians 4:6-9)*

Brothers and sisters: Have no anxiety at all, but in everything, by prayer and petition, with thanksgiving, make your requests known to God. Then the peace of God that surpasses all understanding will guard your hearts and minds in Christ Jesus. Finally, brothers and sisters, whatever is true, whatever is honorable, whatever is just, whatever is pure, whatever is lovely, whatever is gracious, if there is any excellence and if there is anything worthy of praise, think about these things. Keep on doing what you have learned and received and heard and seen in me. Then the **God of peace** will be with you.

The word of the Lord. **Thanks be to God.**

Gospel *(Matthew 21:33-43)*

A reading from the holy Gospel according to Matthew.
Glory to you, O Lord.

Jesus said to the chief priests and the **elders** of the people: "Hear another parable. There was a landowner who planted a vineyard, put a hedge around it, dug a **wine press** in it, and built a tower. Then he leased it to tenants and went on a journey. When vintage time drew near, he sent his servants to the tenants to obtain his produce. But the tenants seized the servants and one they beat, another they killed, and a third they stoned. Again he sent other servants, more numerous than the first ones, but they treated them in the same way. Finally, he sent his son to them, thinking, 'They will respect my son.' But when the tenants saw the son, they said to one another, 'This is the heir. Come, let us kill him and acquire his inheritance.' They seized him, threw him out of the vineyard, and killed him. What will the owner of the vineyard do to those tenants when he comes?" They answered him, "He will put those wretched men to a wretched death and lease his vineyard to other tenants who will give him the produce at the proper times." Jesus said to them, "Did you never read in the Scriptures:

> *The stone that the builders rejected*
> > *has become the cornerstone;*
> *by the Lord has this been done,*
> > *and it is wonderful in our eyes?*

Therefore, I say to you, the kingdom of God will be taken away from you and given to a people that will produce its fruit."

The Gospel of the Lord. **Praise to you, Lord Jesus Christ.**

A **ruin** is a dry, lifeless place where nothing grows. It is ignored and brings nothing good to the community.

Briers are wild thorny plants that grow in untended fields. They discourage both people and animals from entering the field.

Justice promotes peace. But injustice brings about **bloodshed** and destruction. We must work for justice in our world.

God of peace is a name for God. When we follow what God teaches, peace becomes possible—not only peace between enemies, but peace in our hearts as well.

Elders are older people who have a great deal of life experience and wisdom. They hold a position of respect in society and they help us make wise choices.

A **wine press** is used to squeeze the juice from grapes, so that wine can be made from the juice. Presses are also used to make cider from apples and olive oil from olives.

OCTOBER 15
28th Sunday
in Ordinary Time

First Reading *(Isaiah 25:6-10a)*

On this **mountain** the LORD of hosts
  will provide for all peoples
a **feast** of rich food and choice wines,
  juicy, rich food and pure, choice wines.
On this mountain he will destroy
  the veil that veils all peoples,
the web that is woven over all nations;
  he will destroy death forever.
The Lord GOD will wipe away
  the tears from every face;
the reproach of his people he will remove
  from the whole earth; for the LORD has spoken.
  On that day it will be said:
"Behold our God, to whom we looked to save us!
  This is the LORD for whom we looked;
  let us rejoice and be glad that he has saved us!"
For the hand of the LORD will rest on this mountain.

The word of the Lord. **Thanks be to God.**

Responsorial Psalm *(Psalm 23:1-3a, 3b-4, 5, 6)*

R. **I shall live in the house of the Lord
all the days of my life.**

The LORD is my shepherd; I shall not want.
  In verdant pastures he gives me repose.
Beside restful waters he leads me;
  he refreshes my soul. R.
He guides me in right paths
  for his name's sake.
Even though I walk in the dark valley
  I fear no evil; for you are at my side.
with your rod and your staff
  that give me courage. R.
You spread the table before me
  in the sight of my foes;
you anoint my head with oil;
  my cup overflows. R.

> R. **I shall live in the house of the Lord
> all the days of my life.**
>
> Only goodness and kindness follow me
>   all the days of my life;
> and I shall dwell in the house of the LORD
>   for years to come. R.

Second Reading *(Philippians 4:12-14, 19-20)*

Brothers and sisters: I know how to live in humble circumstances; I know also how to live with abundance. In every circumstance and in all things I have learned the secret of being well fed and of going hungry, of living in abundance and of being in need. I can do all things in him who strengthens me. Still, it was kind of you to share in my distress.

My God will fully supply whatever you need, in accord with his glorious riches in Christ Jesus. To our God and Father, glory forever and ever. **Amen**.

The word of the Lord. **Thanks be to God.**

Gospel *(Matthew 22:1-14)*

The shorter version ends with the asterisks.

A reading from the holy Gospel according to Matthew.
Glory to you, O Lord.

Jesus again in reply spoke to the chief priests and elders of the people in **parables**, saying, "The **kingdom of heaven** may be likened to a king who gave a wedding feast for his son. He dispatched his servants to summon the invited guests to the feast, but they refused to come. A second time he sent other servants, saying, 'Tell those invited: "Behold, I have prepared my banquet, my calves and fattened cattle are killed, and everything is ready; come to the feast." ' Some ignored the invitation and went away, one to his farm, another to his business. The rest laid hold of his servants, mistreated them, and killed them. The king was enraged and sent his troops, destroyed those murderers, and burned their city. Then he said to his servants, 'The feast is ready, but those who were invited were not worthy to come. Go out, therefore, into the main roads and invite to the feast whomever you find.' The servants went out into the streets and gathered all they found, bad and good alike, and the hall was filled with **guests**.

* * *

But when the king came in to meet the guests, he saw a man there not dressed in a wedding garment. The king said to him, 'My friend, how is it that you came in here without a wedding garment?' But he was reduced to silence. Then the king said to his attendants, 'Bind his hands and feet, and cast him into the darkness outside, where there will be wailing and grinding of teeth.' Many are invited, but few are chosen."

The Gospel of the Lord. **Praise to you, Lord Jesus Christ.**

In the Bible, the people of God often encounter God up a **mountain**. The mountain is a place that is close to God. It is where God gave Moses the Ten Commandments. Sometimes Jesus also went up the mountain to meet God, such as when he was transfigured.

A **feast** or banquet with delicious foods and fine wines represents the joyful celebration that God prepares for us. The Eucharist gives us a taste of this final celebration.

Amen is a Hebrew word that means "so be it" or "I know this is true." By saying "Amen" after hearing or saying a prayer, we are agreeing with what it says.

Parables are brief stories or wise sayings that Jesus used when he was teaching. Jesus used everyday situations to help his listeners understand what he meant. The parables invite us to change our lives and turn to God.

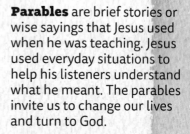

Jesus came to tell us about the **kingdom of heaven**, where people will live peacefully, respecting others and recognizing God as the source of all our joys.

When we are **guests** at a celebration, we wear our best clothes and often bring a gift. This shows that the host and the occasion are important to us. It is the same when we come to Sunday Mass. We come prepared to celebrate, to be attentive, and to share our gifts with God and the community.

OCTOBER 22

29th Sunday in Ordinary Time

First Reading *(Isaiah 45:1, 4-6)*

Thus says the LORD to his **anointed**, Cyrus,
    whose right hand I grasp,
subduing nations before him,
    and making kings run in his service,
opening doors before him
    and leaving the gates unbarred:
For the sake of Jacob, my servant,
    of Israel, my chosen one,
I have called you by your name,
    giving you a title, though you knew me not.
I am the LORD and **there is no other**,
    there is no God besides me.
It is I who arm you, though you know me not,
    so that toward the rising and the setting of the sun
    people may know that there is none besides me.
I am the LORD, there is no other.

The word of the Lord. **Thanks be to God.**

Responsorial Psalm *(Psalm 96:1, 3, 4-5, 7-8, 9-10)*

R. **Give the Lord glory and honor.**

Sing to the LORD a new song;
    sing to the LORD, all you lands.
Tell his glory among the nations;
    among all peoples, his wondrous deeds. R.
For great is the LORD and highly to be praised;
    awesome is he, beyond all gods.
For all the gods of the nations are things of nought,
    but the LORD made the heavens. R.
Give to the LORD, you families of nations,
    give to the LORD glory and praise;
    give to the LORD the glory due his name!
Bring gifts, and enter his courts. R.
Worship the LORD, in holy attire;
    tremble before him, all the earth;
say among the nations: The LORD is king,
    he governs the peoples with equity. R.

Second Reading *(1 Thessalonians 1:1-5b)*

Paul, Silvanus, and Timothy to the church of the Thessalonians in God the Father and the Lord Jesus Christ: grace to you and peace. We give thanks to God always for all of you, remembering you in our prayers, unceasingly calling to mind your work of faith and labor of love and endurance in hope of our Lord Jesus Christ, before our God and Father, knowing, brothers and sisters loved by God, how you were chosen. For our gospel did not come to you in word alone, but also in power and in the Holy Spirit and with much conviction.

The word of the Lord. **Thanks be to God.**

Gospel *(Matthew 22:15-21)*

A reading from the holy Gospel according to Matthew.
Glory to you, O Lord.

The Pharisees went off and plotted how they might entrap Jesus in speech. They sent their disciples to him, with the Herodians, saying, "Teacher, we know that you are a truthful man and that you teach the way of God in accordance with the truth. And you are not concerned with anyone's opinion, for you do not regard a person's status. Tell us, then, what is your opinion: Is it lawful to pay the census tax to Caesar or not?" Knowing their malice, Jesus said, "Why are you testing me, you **hypocrites**? Show me the coin that pays the census tax." Then they handed him the **Roman coin**. He said to them, "Whose image is this and whose inscription?" They replied, "Caesar's." At that he said to them, "Then repay to Caesar what belongs to Caesar and to God what belongs to God."

The Gospel of the Lord. **Praise to you, Lord Jesus Christ.**

To anoint means to bless with oil. In the Bible it can also mean to give someone a mission, an important job. Christians are **anointed** at baptism and confirmation, we anoint people when they are very sick, and priests and bishops are anointed at their ordination: our mission is to live as Jesus taught us.

At the time of Isaiah, neighboring peoples worshipped different gods. But through Isaiah the Lord told Israel that God wasn't just better than the other gods—God is the only God, and **there is no other** at all.

To judge with **equity** is to be fair to everyone. The psalmist praises God for his fairness to all people on earth.

Saint Paul wrote two letters to the **Thessalonians**, Christians who lived in Thessalonica, in Greece. In this letter Paul praises them and encourages them to continue to love one another.

Hypocrites are people who say one thing but do another. They may say they love God, but they don't act in a loving way. Such behavior demeans the person, hurts others and insults God.

This **Roman coin** was worth one day's pay. It had the profile of the Roman emperor stamped on one side of it.

OCTOBER 29

30th Sunday in Ordinary Time

First Reading *(Exodus 22:20-26)*

Thus says the LORD: "You shall not molest or **oppress** an alien, for you were once aliens yourselves in the land of Egypt. You shall not **wrong** any widow or orphan. If ever you wrong them and they cry out to me, I will surely hear their cry. My wrath will flare up, and I will kill you with the sword; then your own wives will be widows, and your children orphans.

"If you lend money to one of your poor neighbors among my people, you shall not act like an **extortioner** toward him by demanding interest from him. If you take your neighbor's cloak as a pledge, you shall return it to him before sunset; for this cloak of his is the only covering he has for his body. What else has he to sleep in? If he cries out to me, I will hear him; for I am compassionate."

The word of the Lord. **Thanks be to God.**

Responsorial Psalm *(Psalm 18:2-3, 3-4, 47, 51)*

℟. **I love you, Lord, my strength.**

I love you, O LORD, my strength,
    O LORD, my rock, my fortress, my deliverer. ℟.
My God, my rock of refuge,
    my shield, the horn of my salvation, my stronghold!
Praised be the LORD, I exclaim,
    and I am safe from my enemies. ℟.
The LORD lives and blessed be my rock!
    Extolled be God my savior.
You who gave great victories to your king
    and showed kindness to your anointed. ℟.

Second Reading *(1 Thessalonians 1:5c-10)*

Brothers and sisters: You know what sort of people we were among you for your sake. And you became imitators of us and of the Lord, receiving the word in great affliction, with **joy** from the Holy Spirit, so that you became a model for all the believers in Macedonia and in Achaia. For from you the word of the Lord has sounded forth not only in Macedonia and in Achaia, but in every place your faith in God has gone forth, so that we have no need to say anything. For they themselves openly declare about us what sort of reception we had among you, and how you turned to God from idols to serve the living and true God and to await his Son from heaven, whom he raised from the dead, Jesus, who delivers us from the coming wrath.

The word of the Lord. **Thanks be to God.**

Gospel *(Matthew 22:34-40)*

A reading from the holy Gospel according to Matthew.
Glory to you, O Lord.

When the **Pharisees** heard that Jesus had silenced the **Sadducees**, they gathered together, and one of them, a scholar of the law tested him by asking, "Teacher, which commandment in the law is the greatest?" He said to him, "You shall love the Lord, your God, with all your heart, with all your soul, and with all your mind. This is the greatest and the first commandment. The second is like it: You shall love your **neighbor** as yourself. The whole law and the prophets depend on these two commandments."

The Gospel of the Lord. **Praise to you, Lord Jesus Christ.**

Key Words

To **oppress** or **wrong** someone is to take advantage of their work for personal benefit. The result is workers who are poorly paid and cannot provide the necessities of life for their families, while the oppressor grows richer and stronger.

An **extortioner** is someone who lends money and charges excessive interest on the loan. Repaying the loan can be a hardship for someone already living in poverty, such as the widows and orphans in the Bible, and can leave them in even greater need than before.

True **joy** is a gift of the Holy Spirit. It is a feeling that stays with us even if we have problems or troubles. Saint Paul tells us the source of this joy is knowing that we are God's beloved children.

The **Pharisees** and the **Sadducees** were people who belonged to two Jewish religious sects. Pharisees were very strict and believed religion consisted in obeying the rules, sometimes forgetting that love is the greatest rule. The Sadducees did not believe in the resurrection of the dead.

The word **neighbor** is related to the word "nigh" which means "near." When Jesus says to love our neighbor, though, he doesn't mean just the people who are close to us—Jesus commands us to think of everyone as our neighbor and to love everyone as we love ourselves.

First Reading *(Revelation 7:2-4, 9-14)*

I, John, saw another angel come up from the East, holding the seal of the living God. He cried out in a loud voice to the four angels who were given power to damage the land and the sea, "Do not damage the land or the sea or the trees until we put the seal on the foreheads of the servants of our God." I heard the number of those who had been marked with the seal, one hundred and forty-four thousand marked from every tribe of the children of Israel.

After this I had a vision of a great multitude, which no one could count, from every nation, race, people, and tongue. They stood before the throne and before the Lamb, wearing white robes and holding palm branches in their hands. They cried out in a loud voice:

"Salvation comes from our God, who is seated on the throne,
and from the Lamb."

All the angels stood around the throne and around the elders and the four living creatures. They prostrated themselves before the throne, worshiped God, and exclaimed:

"Amen. Blessing and glory, wisdom and thanksgiving,
honor, power, and might
be to our God forever and ever. Amen."

Then one of the elders spoke up and said to me, "Who are these **wearing white robes**, and where did they come from?" I said to him, "My lord, you are the one who knows." He said to me, "These are the ones who have survived the time of great distress; they have washed their robes and made them white in the Blood of the Lamb."

The word of the Lord. **Thanks be to God.**

Responsorial Psalm *(Psalm 24:1bc-2, 3-4ab, 5-6)*

R. **Lord, this is the people that longs to see your face.**

The LORD's are the earth and its fullness;
the world and those who dwell in it.
For he founded it upon the seas
and established it upon the rivers. R.

> Who can ascend the mountain of the LORD?
> or who may stand in his holy place?
> One whose hands are sinless, whose heart is clean,
> who desires not what is vain. R.
> He shall receive a blessing from the LORD,
> a reward from God his savior.
> Such is the race that seeks him,
> that seeks the face of the God of Jacob. R.

Second Reading *(1 John 3:1-3)*

Beloved: See what love the Father has bestowed on us that we may be called the children of God. Yet so we are. The reason the world does not know us is that it did not know him. Beloved, we are God's children now; what we shall be has not yet been revealed. We do know that when it is revealed we shall be like him, for we shall see him as he is. Everyone who has this hope based on him makes himself pure, as he is pure.

The word of the Lord. **Thanks be to God.**

Gospel *(Matthew 5:1-12a)*

A reading from the holy Gospel according to Matthew.
Glory to you, O Lord.

When Jesus saw the crowds, he went **up the mountain**, and after he had sat down, his disciples came to him. He began to teach them, saying:
"Blessed are the poor in spirit,
for theirs is the Kingdom of heaven.
Blessed are they who mourn,
for they will be comforted.
Blessed are the meek,
for they will inherit the land.
Blessed are they who hunger and thirst for righteousness,
for they will be satisfied.
Blessed are the merciful,
for they will be shown mercy.
Blessed are the clean of heart,
for they will see God.

Blessed are the peacemakers,
    for they will be called children of God.
Blessed are they who are persecuted for the sake of righteousness,
    for theirs is the Kingdom of heaven.
Blessed are you when they insult you and persecute you and utter every kind of evil against you falsely because of me. Rejoice and be glad, for your reward will be great in heaven."

The Gospel of the Lord. **Praise to you, Lord Jesus Christ.**

Key Words

All Saints is the day we remember all the saints who live with God in heaven. This includes all the men and women we officially call saints, but also all the holy people whose sainthood is known only by God.

Revelation is the last book of the Bible. Its messages are hidden in symbols that often seem very strange to us. Everything has a hidden meaning—the colors, numbers, even the dragons and monsters. The early Christians understood what the writer was trying to tell them. They were facing difficult times, but Revelation told them not to be discouraged, for in the end, Jesus would win over all their enemies.

Those **wearing white robes** are the ones who belong to Jesus. When you were baptized, you were dressed in a white garment to show that you too are part of his people.

Just as Moses went **up a mountain** to get the Ten Commandments from God. Jesus goes up the mountain to proclaim his Beatitudes ("Blessed are..."). These Beatitudes show us how to live today and help us move even more deeply into God's love.

NOVEMBER 5
31st Sunday in Ordinary Time

First Reading (*Malachi 1:14b-2:2b, 8-10*)

A great King am I, says the LORD of hosts,
   and my name will be feared among the nations.
And now, O priests, this commandment is for you:
   If you do not listen,
if you do not lay it to heart,
   to give glory to my name, says the LORD of hosts,
I will send a curse upon you
   and of your blessing I will make a curse.
You have turned aside from the way,
   and have caused many to falter by your instruction;
you have made void the covenant of **Levi**,
   says the LORD of hosts.
I, therefore, have made you contemptible
   and base before all the people,
since you do not keep my ways,
   but show partiality in your decisions.
Have we not all the one father?
   Has not the one God created us?
Why then do we break faith with one another,
   violating the covenant of our fathers?

The word of the Lord. **Thanks be to God.**

Responsorial Psalm (*Psalm 131:1, 2, 3*)

R. **In you, Lord, I have found my peace.**

O LORD, my heart is not proud,
   nor are my eyes haughty;
I busy not myself with great things,
   nor with things too sublime for me. R.
Nay rather, I have stilled and quieted
   my soul like a weaned child.
Like a weaned child on its mother's lap,
   so is my soul within me. R.
O Israel, hope in the LORD,
   both now and forever. R.

Second Reading (1 Thessalonians 2:7b-9, 13)

Brothers and sisters: We were gentle among you, as a nursing mother cares for her children. With such affection for you, we were determined to share with you not only the gospel of God, but our very selves as well, so dearly beloved had you become to us. You recall, brothers and sisters, our toil and drudgery. Working night and day in order not to burden any of you, we proclaimed to you the gospel of God.

And for this reason we too give thanks to God unceasingly, that, in receiving the word of God from hearing us, you received not a human word but, as it truly is, the word of God, which is now at work in you who believe.

The word of the Lord. **Thanks be to God.**

Gospel (Matthew 23:1-12)

A reading from the holy Gospel according to Matthew.
Glory to you, O Lord.

Jesus spoke to the crowds and to his disciples, saying, "The scribes and the Pharisees have taken their seat **on the chair of Moses**. Therefore, do and observe all things whatsoever they tell you, but do not follow their example. For they preach but they do not practice. They tie up heavy burdens hard to carry and lay them on people's shoulders, but they will not lift a finger to move them. All their works are performed to be seen. They widen their **phylacteries** and lengthen their tassels. They love places of honor at banquets, seats of honor in synagogues, greetings in marketplaces, and the salutation 'Rabbi.' As for you, do not be called 'Rabbi.' You have but one teacher, and you are all brothers. Call no one on earth your father; you have but one Father in heaven. Do not be called 'Master'; you have but one master, the Christ. The greatest among you must be your servant. Whoever exalts himself will be humbled; but whoever humbles himself will be exalted."

The Gospel of the Lord. **Praise to you, Lord Jesus Christ.**

Key Words

The book of the Prophet **Malachi** was written to try to awaken hope in the people of Israel at a time when religious practice had deteriorated. It was written 515 years before Christ.

....

Levi was one of Jacob's twelve sons and head of one of the twelve tribes of Israel. Levites were of the priestly class and therefore represented the covenant between God and Israel.

....

When Jesus says that the scribes and Pharisees sit **on the chair of Moses**, he is recognizing that their authority to teach goes back to Moses who received the Ten Commandments from God.

....

Phylacteries are small boxes worn by some Jewish men on the left wrist and on the forehead. The boxes contain Biblical texts; they are worn to help the wearer keep God's word always at hand and in mind. Jesus wants us to see that what counts is what is in our heart, and not what we wear on the outside.

First Reading *(Wisdom 6:12-16)*

Resplendent and unfading is wisdom,
>and she is readily perceived by those who love her,
>and found by those who seek her.

She hastens to make herself known in anticipation of their desire;
>whoever watches for her at dawn shall not be disappointed,
>for he shall find her sitting by his gate.

For taking thought of wisdom is the perfection of prudence,
>and whoever for her sake keeps vigil
>shall quickly be free from care;

because she makes her own rounds, seeking those worthy of her,
>and graciously appears to them in the ways,
>and meets them with all solicitude.

The word of the Lord. **Thanks be to God.**

Responsorial Psalm *(Psalm 63:2, 3-4, 5-6, 7-8)*

R̸. **My soul is thirsting for you, O Lord my God.**

O God, you are my God whom I seek;
>for you my flesh pines and my soul thirsts
>like the earth, parched, lifeless and without water. R̸.

Thus have I gazed toward you in the **sanctuary**
>to see your power and your glory,
>for your kindness is a greater good than life;
>my lips shall glorify you. R̸.

Thus will I bless you while I live;
>lifting up my hands, I will call upon your name.
>As with the riches of a banquet shall my soul be satisfied,
>and with exultant lips my mouth shall praise you. R̸.

I will remember you upon my couch,
>and through the night-watches I will meditate on you:
>you are my help,
>and in the shadow of your wings I shout for joy. R̸.

Second Reading *(1 Thessalonians 4:13-18)*

The shorter version ends at the asterisks.

We do not want you to be unaware, brothers and sisters, about those who have fallen asleep, so that you may not grieve like the rest, who have no hope. For if we believe that Jesus died and rose, so too will God, through Jesus, bring with him those who have fallen asleep.

* * *

Indeed, we tell you this, on the word of the Lord, that we who are alive, who are left until the coming of the Lord, will surely not precede those who have fallen asleep. For the Lord himself, with a word of command, with the voice of an archangel and with the trumpet of God, will come down from heaven, and the dead in Christ will rise first. Then we who are alive, who are left, will be caught up together with them in the clouds to meet the Lord in the air. Thus we shall always be with the Lord. Therefore, console one another with these words.

The word of the Lord. **Thanks be to God.**

Gospel *(Matthew 25:1-13)*

A reading from the holy Gospel according to Matthew.
Glory to you, O Lord.

Jesus told his disciples this parable: "The kingdom of heaven will be like ten virgins who took their **lamps** and went out to meet the bridegroom. Five of them were foolish and five were wise. The foolish ones, when taking their lamps, brought no oil with them, but the wise brought flasks of oil with their lamps. Since the bridegroom was long delayed, they all became drowsy and fell asleep. At midnight, there was a cry, 'Behold, the bridegroom! Come out to meet him!' Then all those virgins got up and **trimmed** their lamps. The foolish ones said to the wise, 'Give us some of your oil, for our lamps are going out.' But the wise ones replied, 'No, for there may not be enough for us and you. Go instead to the merchants and buy some for yourselves.' While they went off to buy it, the bridegroom came and those who were ready went into the wedding feast with him. Then the door was locked. Afterwards the other virgins came and said, 'Lord, Lord, open the door for us!' But he said in reply, 'Amen, I say to you, I do not know you.' Therefore, stay awake, for you know neither the day nor the hour."

The Gospel of the Lord. **Praise to you, Lord Jesus Christ.**

The **book of Wisdom** was written not long before Jesus was born. It urges us to make good decisions in life. It teaches about justice and fairness.

The **sanctuary** is the holiest part of the Jewish temple (from the Latin word *sanctus* that gives us both of the words "holy" and "saint"). In a church, the sanctuary is the place where the word of God is proclaimed and the Eucharist is celebrated.

In the time of Jesus, wedding ceremonies were held at night. Therefore, the bridesmaids needed to have **lamps** ready to light the way when they went to meet the bridegroom. If their lamps went out, there was no other source of light until morning.

The bridesmaids used oil lamps with wicks. The wicks needed to be **trimmed** properly before lighting so that the lamps would burn brightly, cleanly, and not too quickly.

First Reading *(Proverbs 31:10-13, 19-20, 30-31)*

When one finds a worthy wife,
     her value is far beyond pearls.
Her husband, entrusting his heart to her,
     has an unfailing prize.
She brings him good, and not evil,
     all the days of her life.
She obtains **wool and flax**
     and works with loving hands.
She puts her hands to the distaff,
     and her fingers ply the spindle.
She reaches out her hands to the poor,
     and extends her arms to the needy.
Charm is deceptive and beauty fleeting;
     the woman who fears the LORD is to be praised.
Give her a reward for her labors,
     and let her works praise her at the city gates.

The word of the Lord. **Thanks be to God.**

Responsorial Psalm *(Psalm 128:1-2, 3, 4-5)*

R. **Blessed are those who fear the Lord.**

Blessed are you who fear the Lord,
     who walk in his ways!
For you shall eat the fruit of your handiwork;
     blessed shall you be, and favored. R.
Your wife shall be like a fruitful vine
     in the recesses of your home;
Your children like olive plants
     around your table. R.
Behold, thus is the man blessed
     who fears the LORD.
The LORD bless you from Zion:
     may you see the prosperity of Jerusalem
     all the days of your life. R.

Second Reading *(1 Thessalonians 5:1-6)*

Concerning times and seasons, brothers and sisters, you have no need for anything to be written to you. For you yourselves know very well that the day of the Lord will come like a thief at night. When people are saying, "Peace and security," then sudden disaster comes upon them, like labor pains upon a pregnant woman, and they will not escape.

But you, brothers and sisters, are not in **darkness**, for that day to overtake you like a thief. For all of you are children of the **light** and children of the day. We are not of the night or of darkness. Therefore, let us not sleep as the rest do, but let us stay alert and **sober**.

The word of the Lord. **Thanks be to God.**

Gospel *(Matthew 25:14-30)*

For the shorter version, omit the indented parts in brackets.

A reading from the holy Gospel according to Matthew.
Glory to you, O Lord.

Jesus told his disciples this parable: "A man going on a journey called in his servants and entrusted his possessions to them. To one he gave five talents; to another, two; to a third, one—to each according to his ability. Then he went away.

[Immediately the one who received five **talents** went and traded with them, and made another five. Likewise, the one who received two made another two. But the man who received one went off and dug a hole in the ground and buried his master's money.]

"After a long time the master of those servants came back and settled accounts with them. The one who had received five talents came forward bringing the additional five. He said, 'Master, you gave me five talents. See, I have made five more.' His master said to him, 'Well done, my good and **faithful** servant. Since you were faithful in small matters, I will give you great responsibilities. Come, share your master's joy.'

[Then the one who had received two talents also came forward and said, 'Master, you gave me two talents. See, I have made two more.' His master said to him, 'Well done, my good and faithful servant. Since you were faithful in small matters, I will give you great responsibilities. Come, share your master's joy.' Then the one who had received the one talent came forward and said, 'Master, I knew you were a demanding person, harvesting where you did not plant and gathering where you did not scatter; so out of fear I went off and buried your talent in the ground. Here it is back.' His master said to him in reply, 'You wicked, lazy servant! So you knew that I harvest where I did not plant and gather where I did not scatter? Should you not then have put my money in the bank so that I could have got it back with interest on my return? Now then! Take the talent from him and give it to the one with ten. For to everyone who has, more will be given and he will grow rich; but from the one who has not, even what he has will be taken away. And throw this useless servant into the darkness outside, where there will be wailing and grinding of teeth.']"

The Gospel of the Lord. **Praise to you, Lord Jesus Christ.**

The book of Proverbs is a collection of popular sayings and parables filled with advice and wisdom.

Wool and flax are two natural materials that are used in making cloth and ropes, both of which were very important in ancient households. It was the woman's responsibility to spin the yarn and weave the cloth needed in a home.

Light is a symbol of everything good and especially of Jesus, who is the Light of the World. **Darkness** represents evil, especially turning away from God.

To live a **sober** life means to do things in moderation, without excess. If we do not live soberly, then we may be too caught up in our own pleasure and will not pay attention to the needs of others or to the Holy Spirit living within us.

The **talents** in the parable are coins that represent the gifts God has given to each one of us: our intelligence, our memory, our capacity for generosity and kindness. These gifts must be used for the good of all.

To be **faithful** is to be honest and dependable. When someone gives us a task or asks us to keep a secret and we keep our promises, we show that we value that person's friendship.

NOVEMBER 26
**Our Lord Jesus Christ,
King of the Universe**

First Reading *(Ezekiel 34:11-12, 15-17)*

Thus says the Lord GOD: I myself will look after and tend **my sheep**. As a **shepherd** tends his flock when he finds himself among his scattered sheep, so will I tend **my sheep**. I will rescue them from every place where they were scattered when it was cloudy and dark. I myself will pasture my sheep; I myself will give them rest, says the Lord GOD. The lost I will seek out, the strayed I will bring back, the injured I will bind up, the sick I will heal, but the sleek and the strong I will destroy, shepherding them rightly.

As for you, my sheep, says the Lord GOD, I will judge between one sheep and another, between rams and goats.

The word of the Lord. **Thanks be to God.**

Responsorial Psalm *(Psalm 23:1-2, 2-3, 5-6)*

R. **The Lord is my shepherd; there is nothing I shall want.**

The LORD is my shepherd; I shall not want.
    In verdant pastures he gives me repose. R.
Beside restful waters he leads me;
    he refreshes my soul.
He guides me in right paths
    for his name's sake. R.
You spread the table before me
    in the sight of my foes;
you anoint my head with oil;
    my cup overflows. R.
Only goodness and kindness follow me
    all the days of my life;
and I shall dwell in the house of the LORD
    for years to come R.

Second Reading *(1 Corinthians 15:20-26, 28)*

Brothers and sisters: Christ has been raised from the dead, the **firstfruits** of those who have fallen asleep. For since death came through man, the resurrection of the dead came also through man. For just as in Adam all die, so too in Christ shall all be brought to life, but each one in proper order: Christ the firstfruits; then, at his **coming**, those who belong to Christ; then comes the end, when he hands over the kingdom to his God and Father, when he has destroyed every sovereignty and every authority and power. For he must reign until he has put all his enemies under his feet. The last enemy to be destroyed is death. When everything is subjected to him, then the Son himself will also be subjected to the one who subjected everything to him, so that God may be all in all.

The word of the Lord. **Thanks be to God.**

Gospel *(Matthew 25:31-46)*

A reading from the holy Gospel according to Matthew.
Glory to you, O Lord.

Jesus said to his **disciples**: "When the Son of Man comes in his glory, and all the angels with him, he will sit upon his glorious throne, and all the nations will be assembled before him. And he will separate them one from another, as a shepherd separates the sheep from the goats. He will place the sheep on his right and the goats on his left. Then the king will say to those on his right, 'Come, you who are blessed by my Father. Inherit the kingdom prepared for you from the foundation of the world. For I was hungry and you gave me food, I was thirsty and you gave me drink, a stranger and you welcomed me, naked and you clothed me, ill and you cared for me, in prison and you visited me.' Then the righteous will answer him and say, 'Lord, when did we see you hungry and feed you, or thirsty and give you drink? When did we see you a stranger and welcome you, or naked and clothe you? When did we see you ill or in prison, and visit you?' And the king will say to them in reply, 'Amen, I say to you, whatever you did for one of the least brothers of mine, you did for me.' Then he will say to those on his left, 'Depart from me, you accursed, into the eternal fire prepared for the devil and his angels. For I was hungry and you gave me no food, I was thirsty and you gave me no drink, a stranger and you gave me no welcome, naked and you gave me no clothing, ill and in prison, and you did not care for me.' Then they will answer and say, 'Lord, when did we see you hungry or thirsty or a stranger or naked or ill or in prison, and not minister to your needs?' He will answer them, 'Amen, I say to you, what you did not do for one of these least ones, you did not do for me.' And these will go off to eternal punishment, but the righteous to eternal life."

The Gospel of the Lord. **Praise to you, Lord Jesus Christ.**

Key Words

Ezekiel was one of the most important prophets in Israel. He lived during a time when many of the people of Jerusalem were taken prisoner and forced to live in exile, in Babylon. The king and Ezekiel were taken away, too. Ezekiel helped the people follow God's ways even though they were far from home.

God calls his people **my sheep** to show how valuable we are to God. Because they provide wool for clothing as well as meat for food, sheep are very important animals. A community's survival could depend on the safety and health of its sheep.

A **shepherd** is someone who takes care of a flock of sheep. He would spend days or weeks with his flock, sleeping with them and making sure they were always safe. God loves us with the same constant care.

The **Corinthians** were a community of Christians who lived in Corinth, a city in Greece. Saint Paul wrote them several letters, two of which were preserved and are in the Bible.

First fruits were the first crops collected at harvest time. These were offered to God. Saint Paul tells us that Jesus is the first fruits of salvation, the first to die and rise again.

Christ's **coming** or advent is his return at the end of time. All history is longing for Christ's return, when God's plan of salvation will be complete.

A **disciple** is a person who follows the teachings of a master and helps to spread these teachings. Jesus was such a master; he had many disciples, including us.

Morning Prayers

A Child's Prayer for Morning

Now, before I run to play,
let me not forget to pray
to God who kept me through the night
and waked me with the morning light.
Help me, Lord, to love you more
than I have ever loved before.
In my work and in my play
please be with me through the day.
Amen.

Morning Prayer

Dear God, we thank you for this day.
We thank you for our families and friends.
We thank you for our classmates.
Be with us as we work and play today.
Help us always to be kind to each other.
We pray in the name of the Father,
and of the Son and of the Holy Spirit.
Amen.

Heather Reid, *Let's Pray! Prayers for the Elementary Classroom* (Novalis, 2006).

Angel of God

Angel of God, my guardian dear,
to whom God's love entrusts me here,
ever this day be at my side,
to light and guard, to rule and guide.
Amen.

Evening Prayers

Children's Bedtime Prayer

Now I lay me down to sleep,
I pray you, Lord, your child to keep.
Your love will guard me through the night
and wake me with the morning light. Amen.

Child's Evening Prayer

I hear no voice, I feel no touch,
I see no glory bright;
but yet I know that God is near,
in darkness as in light.
He watches ever by my side,
and hears my whispered prayer:
the Father for his little child
both night and day does care.

God, Hear My Prayer

God in heaven hear my prayer,
keep me in your loving care.
Be my guide in all I do,
bless all those who love me too.
Amen.

Mealtime Prayers

Grace before Meals

Bless us, O Lord,
and these your gifts
which we are about to receive
from your bounty.
Through Christ our Lord. Amen.

....

For food in a world where many walk in hunger,
for friends in a world where many walk alone,
for faith in a world where many walk in fear,
we give you thanks, O God. Amen.

....

God is great, God is good!
Let us thank God for our food. Amen.

....

Be present at our table, Lord.
Be here and everywhere adored.
Your creatures bless
and grant that we may feast
in paradise with you. Amen.

Grace after Meals

We give you thanks, Almighty God, for these
and all the benefits we receive from your bounty.
Through Christ our Lord. Amen.

....

Blessed be the name of the Lord.
Now and forever. Amen.

Prayers for Family

Family Prayer

Father, what love you have given us.
May we love as you would have us love.
Teach us to be kind to each other,
patient and gentle with one another.
Help us to bear all things together,
to see in our love, your love,
through Christ our Lord. Amen.

World Meeting of Families Prayer

God and Father of us all,
in Jesus, your Son and our Savior,
you have made us your sons and daughters
in the family of the Church.
May your grace and love help our families
in every part of the world be united to one another
in fidelity to the Gospel.
May the example of the Holy Family,
with the aid of your Holy Spirit,
guide all families, especially those most troubled,
to be homes of communion and prayer
and to always seek your truth and live in your love.
Through Christ our Lord. Amen.
Jesus, Mary, and Joseph, Pray for us!

Prayer of Gratitude for a Family

Loving God,
Thank you for the gift of my family.
   (Pause to name each person in the family.)
Thank you for the times we have to be together.
   (Pause to name a particular way of being together.)
Thank you for the ways in which we care for each other.
   (Pause to name a specific act of kindness.)
May the joy and affection we share increase each
   and every day.
With gratitude for your bountiful love, I pray. Amen.

Kathy Hendricks, *Pocket Prayers for Parents*
(Twenty-Third Publications, 2013).

More Prayers

Prayer for Friends

Loving God, you are the best friend we can have.
We ask today that you help us to be good friends
    to each other.
Help us to be fair, kind, and unselfish.
Keep our friends safe and happy.
Bless us and bless all friends in this community.
We pray in the name of Jesus,
who was always the friend of children. Amen.

Heather Reid, *Let's Pray! Prayers for the Elementary Classroom* (Novalis, 2006).

Prayer for the Birthday Child

May God bless you with every good gift
and surround you with love and happiness.
May Jesus be your friend and guide
all the days of your life.
May the Spirit of God guide your footsteps
in the path of truth. Amen.

Prayer for Student / Teacher who is Sick

Gracious God, _____ is sick right now.
We pray for (him/her/them) and ask that they get
better quickly and be able to return to us. Bless
all nurses, doctors and everyone who cares for
people who are ill. May all sick people find comfort
through their families and friends. We ask this in
the name of Jesus, who healed many people. Amen.

Heather Reid, *Let's Pray! Prayers for the Elementary Classroom* (Novalis, 2006).

When Someone Has Died

Lord God, hear our cries.
Grant us comfort in our sadness,
gently wipe away our tears,
and give us courage in the days ahead.
We ask this through Christ our Lord. Amen.

Daily Prayers for School

Prayer for the Beginning of the School Day

God of wisdom,
you call us to grow in your grace
with hearts to love you,
with souls open to you,
with minds to learn from you.
Help us to see beyond distractions
and keep our vision clear—
a vision of your reign.
Amen.

Prayer at the Closing of the School Day

Loving God,
our creator, our friend, our companion,
bless our journey of learning.
Refresh our souls and renew our spirits.
Lead us in paths of wisdom,
compassion and understanding.
Bless us with an enduring love of learning.
May the Holy Spirit flow freely
Through the classrooms and halls of our school,
through the rooms and gardens of our home,
through our churches and our nation.
We make this prayer in the name of Jesus.
Amen.

Lisa Freemantle and Les Miller, *Words for the Journey: Ten-Minute Prayer Services for Teachers and Administrators* (Novalis, 2009).

Morning Prayer for the First Day of School

+ In the name of the Father, and of the Son, and of the Holy Spirit. Amen.

INTRODUCTION: *Today is the first day of school! We ask God to bless our new school year, that we will learn and grow in many ways this year. Today's reading talks about the importance of wisdom. The writer prayed for this gift, and it was given to him. Like him, let us ask God for the gifts of wisdom and understanding.*

A READING FROM THE BOOK OF WISDOM (7:7-9, 10, 14):

I prayed, and understanding was given me; I called on God, and the spirit of wisdom came to me. I preferred her to sceptres and thrones, and I accounted wealth as nothing in comparison with her. Neither did I liken to her any priceless gem, because all gold is but a little sand in her sight, and I chose to have her rather than light, because her radiance never ceases.

For it is an unfailing treasure for mortals; those who get it obtain friendship with God, commended for the gifts that come from instruction.
The word of the Lord. **Thanks be to God.**

Let us pray:
Dear God,
you are the source of all wisdom and holiness.
Bless each one of us as we begin this new school year.
Help us to grow in wisdom and love.
We ask this through Christ our Lord. **Amen.**

Let us pray the prayer that Jesus taught us:
Our Father, who art in heaven...

+ In the name of the Father, and of the Son, and of the Holy Spirit. Amen.

"Morning Prayer for the First Day of School" and "Morning Prayer for the Last Day of School" are taken from *Prayers for the School Year*, Rosanna Golino (Ottawa: Novalis, 2005).

Morning Prayer for the Last Day of School

+ In the name of the Father, and of the Son, and of the Holy Spirit. Amen.

INTRODUCTION: *We have had a very busy and successful school year. For these things, we thank God with all our hearts. And as Saint Paul tells us today, let us be joyful, prayerful, thankful people, carrying God's love and peace wherever we go.*

A READING FROM THE FIRST LETTER OF PAUL TO THE THESSALONIANS (5:16-23)

Rejoice always, pray without ceasing, give thanks in all circumstances; for this is the will of God in Christ Jesus for you. Do not quench the Spirit. Do not despise the words of prophets, but test everything; hold fast to what is good; abstain from every form of evil.

May the God of peace himself sanctify you entirely; and may your spirit and soul and body be kept sound and blameless at the coming of our Lord Jesus Christ. The grace of our Lord Jesus Christ be with you.
The word of the Lord. **Thanks be to God.**

Let us pray.
℞. **Lord, we praise and thank you.**

For all the good things that have happened this year: ℞.

For our teachers, families, parish, and friends: ℞.

For the times we shared, both good and hard times: ℞.

For the gift of summer vacation: ℞.

For all the gifts you have given us: ℞.

Let us pray the prayer that Jesus taught us:
Our Father, who art in heaven...

+ In the name of the Father, and of the Son, and of the Holy Spirit. Amen.

The Rosary

In the Rosary we focus on 20 events or mysteries in the life and death of Jesus and meditate on how we share with Mary in the saving work of Christ. Reading a relevant passage from the Bible can help us to understand better a particular mystery of the Rosary. The Bible references below are suggestions; other biblical texts can also be used for meditation.

- Begin the Rosary at the crucifix by praying the Apostles' Creed
- At each large bead, pray the Lord's Prayer
- At each small bead, pray the Hail Mary
- At the first three beads it is customary to pray a Hail Mary for each of the gifts of faith, hope, and love
- For each mystery, begin with the Lord's Prayer, then recite the Hail Mary ten times, and end with Glory Be to the Father.

THE FIVE JOYFUL MYSTERIES:

The Annunciation
(Luke 1:26-38)

The Visitation (Luke 1:39-56)

The Nativity (Luke 2:1-20)

The Presentation
(Luke 2:22-38)

The Finding in the Temple
(Luke 2:41-52)

THE FIVE MYSTERIES OF LIGHT:

The Baptism in the Jordan
(Matthew 3.:3-17)

The Wedding at Cana
(John 2:1-12)

The Proclamation of the Kingdom (Mark 1:15)

The Transfiguration
(Luke 9:28-36)

The First Eucharist
(Matthew 26:26-29)

THE FIVE SORROWFUL MYSTERIES:

The Agony in the Garden
(Matthew 26:36-46)

The Scourging at the Pillar
(Matthew 27:20-26)

The Crowning with Thorns
(Matthew 27:27-30)

The Carrying of the Cross
(Matthew 27:31-33)

The Crucifixion
(Matthew 27:34-54)

THE FIVE GLORIOUS MYSTERIES:

The Resurrection
(John 20:1-18)

The Ascension (Acts 1:9-11)

The Descent of the Holy Spirit
(John 20:19-23)

The Assumption of Mary
(John 11:26)

The Crowning of Mary
(Philippians 2:1-11)

Sacraments:
A Gift from God

Sacraments are rituals through which we receive God's grace. Grace is the gift of God's love and strength, given freely to us to help us lead good and just lives. Sacraments always involve signs appealing to our senses that point to God's saving presence in our lives. Baptism requires water, for example, and when we are confirmed, we are anointed with a special oil called chrism.

The seven sacraments of the Catholic Church are **Baptism, Reconciliation**, **Eucharist**, **Confirmation**, **Marriage**, **Holy Orders** and the **Anointing of the Sick**.

Sometimes you will hear people refer to **Sacraments of Initiation**, **Sacraments of Healing**, and **Sacraments of Service**.

The **Sacraments of Initiation**—Baptism, Eucharist and Confirmation—help welcome us into a life of faith.

The **Sacraments of Healing** are Reconciliation and the Anointing of the Sick. Reconciliation helps us when our actions have injured our relationship with God, while the Anointing of the Sick helps us physically, mentally and spiritually when we face illness and suffering.

The **Sacraments of Service**—Marriage and Holy Orders (priesthood)—are linked to our call to serve others.

The sacraments of Baptism, Confirmation and Holy Orders can only be received once. As Catholics, we believe that when these sacraments are received, they leave a lasting mark—or seal— on the soul.

A Young Person's Examination of Conscience

These questions are based on the Ten Commandments and can be used in preparation of the Sacrament of Reconciliation.

1. God Comes First

- Did I pray each day?
- Did I act with respect in church?
- Did I participate at Mass?

2. God's Name Is Holy

- Did I always use God's name in the right way?
- Did I treat and talk about holy things with respect?

3. God's Day Is Holy

- Did I go to Mass on Sundays and Holy Days?
- Did I miss Mass through my own fault?

4. Honor Mom & Dad

- Did I obey my parents?
- Did I treat them with respect?
- Was I obedient and respectful to my teachers?

5. Do Not Kill

- Have I been kind to my siblings and friends?
- Did I hit or hurt anyone?
- Did I harm anyone with mean or cruel words?

6. Be Pure

- Were my thoughts and actions good and pure?
- Have I been careful to watch good movies and TV shows?

7. Do Not Steal

- Have I always been honest?
- Did I take anything that doesn't belong to me?

8. Do Not Lie

- Have I always told the truth?
- Have I spread rumors?
- Have I been quiet about something when I should have spoken up?

9. Do Not Want Other People
and
10. Do Not Want Their Things

- Have I been satisfied with what I have?
- Have I been jealous of another's things, toys, or belongings?
- Am I thankful for what I have?

The Liturgical Year

The readings for Sunday Mass and feast days change according to the liturgical calendar.

WHAT IS THE LITURGICAL YEAR?

Throughout the year, Christians celebrate together important moments in Jesus' life. This is the liturgical year. There are five seasons: Advent, Christmas, Lent, Easter and Ordinary Time.

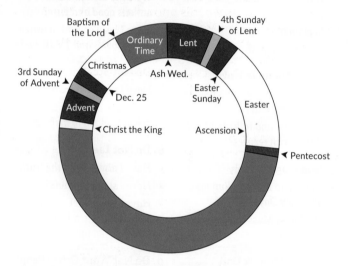

Advent is a time of waiting. It begins 4 Sundays before Christmas. We prepare to welcome Jesus.

Christmas time celebrates the life of Jesus from his birth to his baptism. It includes Epiphany: Jesus welcomes the whole world.

During the 40 days of **Lent** we prepare for the great feast of Easter, the most important moment of the year.

Easter time is a season to celebrate Jesus' victory over death. It lasts from Easter Sunday to Pentecost, when the Holy Spirit comes upon the disciples.

The season in green above is called **Ordinary Time** because the Sundays are arranged using 'ordinal numbers.' It recounts many of the things Jesus did and said during his lifetime.

YEAR A *and the* GOSPEL *of* MATTHEW

The Gospels of Matthew, Mark, and Luke are known as the synoptic gospels, a name which refers to the fact that these three books of the New Testament contain similar material on the life and ministry of Jesus.

Each year, the gospel we hear on the majority of the Sundays in Ordinary Time that year rotates through these three books. This year (2016-2017) is what is known as Year A, the year which focuses on the Gospel of Matthew.

The Gospel of Matthew is the first book of the New Testament. It was written around 85 AD in one of the cities of Syria or Palestine. We do not know who the author was, but our tradition associates him with Saint Matthew the tax collector in Matthew 9.9.

This Gospel tells us how Jesus, who had been rejected by Israel, sends his disciples to preach his Gospel to the whole world. The Gospel tells us about the Kingdom of God which God gives us, and teaches us how to live our lives.

Celebrating Our Faith throughout the Week

As Mass ends, the priest dismisses us with one of several prayers: "Go forth, the Mass is ended," for example, or "Go and announce the Gospel of the Lord." As people of faith, we are called to carry all that we have celebrated at Mass out into our daily lives.
There are several ways to do this:

- Prepare for Mass by reading the coming Sunday's first and second readings, the Psalm and the gospel in advance, so that you are familiar with what you will hear at Mass. Try imagining yourself in the gospel story, witnessing first-hand the story you will hear. Who might you be? What would your reaction be if you were to hear Jesus tell a parable? How would you feel if you were to witness Jesus perform a miracle? What must it have been like to travel with Jesus and listen to him teach and preach?

- After you have heard the gospel proclaimed at Mass, ask yourself what message or idea really made an impression on you. Think about that throughout the week. If there is a phrase or passage that particularly appealed to you, try reciting it to yourself throughout the week. Think of ways it relates to you and to the world today.

- Listen closely to the priest's homily and ask yourself what you have learned from it. Reflect on that point throughout the week.

- Listen to the Prayer of the Faithful and remember who and what were being prayed for at Mass. Keep these petitions in mind as you say your prayers during the week. As you leave Mass, say to yourself, "This week I will pray for _____."